Eastern Cherokee Fishing

T0307935

CONTEMPORARY AMERICAN INDIAN STUDIES

J. Anthony Paredes, *Series Editor*

Eastern Cherokee Fishing

Heidi M. Altman

THE UNIVERSITY OF ALABAMA PRESS
Tuscaloosa

The University of Alabama Press
Tuscaloosa, Alabama 35487-0380
uapress.ua.edu

Typeface: Bembo

Cover image: Courtesy of the U.S. National Oceanic and Atmospheric
Administration
Cover design: David Nees

Cataloging-in-Publication data is available from the Library of Congress.
ISBN: 978-0-8173-5331-5 (paper)
ISBN: 978-0-8173-1514-6 (cloth)
ISBN: 978-0-8173-8045-8 (electronic)

For their support through this process, this work is dedicated to the two fishermen in my life, my husband, Chris Booker, and son, Dalton; to my mother, Zoë, who grew up among the rivers of western North Carolina; and to my father, Jay, the person who first took me fishing and inspired my love for listening to people talk about fishing.

Contents

Illustrations

Figures

Table

Acknowledgments

Many people helped me to produce this work, and I want to thank them for their time and assistance.

First, and foremost, I want to acknowledge and express many thanks to the members of the Eastern Band of Cherokee Indians for allowing me to spend time in their community to learn about the art of Cherokee fishing.

I must express my deepest appreciation and gratitude for the time given to me by Jerry Wolfe, Cherokee fisherman, for his kind and patient lessons in language, fishing, folklore, and history; to Myrtle Driver, for her mentoring, friendship and fishing expertise; to Charles Taylor, for his remembrances of his grandparents, his assistance in translation, and his patient explanations; to James Bird, for his assistance in establishing the research project in the community; and to Kenneth Maney, for his time and trouble in teaching me about the business of Cherokee fishing.

In addition to the friends I have made in the Cherokee community, I must also acknowledge the support I received from the academic communities of which I am a part. I am extremely grateful to the friends and colleagues who have reviewed drafts of this work, including Martha Macri, Janet Smith, Aram Yengoyan, Leanne Hinton, and Margaret Bender. Tony Paredes and James Bird reviewed this manuscript for the press, and I am grateful for their insights and comments. I owe many thanks to Anne Rogers at Western Carolina University, without whom I would still be floundering. I am grateful also to Lisa Lefler for her support, friendship, and seemingly endless knowledge. Finally, I appreciate the various conversations and correspondence I have had with wildlife biologists, archaeologists, and ichthyologists, including Scott Loftis, Brett Riggs, Art Bogan, and Robert Jenkins.

Archival research at the American Philosophical Society in Philadelphia was funded by a Faculty Research and Creative Activity Grant from Middle Tennessee State University. I greatly appreciate the opportunity and recognize that small intramural grants such as these are often in a precarious position, but they are crucial to the completion of all sorts of small but important research. The staff at the APS also deserves mention for their tireless and enthusiastic assistance.

All of these people have contributed their time and energy to promoting my success, but any mistakes herein are my own, in spite of their best efforts.

Notes on the Transcription
of Cherokee Words in the Text

1. Most of the sounds of Cherokee are found in English, although there are several sounds in English not found in Cherokee. Therefore, for most sounds represented here, I use the Roman alphabet equivalent. A chart of Cherokee sounds and the symbols used to represent them is presented below.
2. The transcriptions throughout this text are properly called phonemic rather than what is commonly called phonetic; that is to say they reflect *meaningful* distinctions between sounds. Proper phonetic transcription involves recording all distinctions in sound, including qualities of breath, tone, pitch, length, and a variety of other features that are not reflected here.
3. Conventions in Cherokee spelling often depend on syllabic writing, which is based on reading knowledge of the syllabary but which does not always lead to correct pronunciation for nonspeakers. Many sources that contain Cherokee words use syllabic spellings, which are usually indicated by hyphenation between regularly shaped, open, consonant-vowel (or sometimes consonant-consonant-vowel) syllables. Syllabic spelling is not used in this text unless it was presented to me in that form by a speaker or from another source.

Vowels in Cherokee

/a/ = the vowel sound in "father"
/e/ = the vowel sound in "say"
/i/ = the vowel sound in "meet"
/o/ = the vowel sound in "both"
/u/ = the vowel sound in "shoe"
/v/ = the nasalized vowel sound in "uh-uh"

Consonants in Cherokee

Single consonants represented here have the same value they have in English: /d/, /g/, /h/, /j/, /k/, /ɪ/, /m/, /n/, /s/, /t/, /y/.

Consonant clusters have the following values:
/hn/ = no exact equivalent in English; breathe out through the nose as pronouncing the /n/.
/tl/ = no exact equivalent in English; place tip of tongue behind teeth and let air flow out side of tongue, then release.
/ts/ or /ch/ = somewhere between the /ch/ and /j/ sound of English.
/kw/ = the "qu" sound in "queen."

I

Introduction

Reminiscences and recollections of fishing have a certain reputation for being exaggerated and far-fetched, and so some might see them as a suitable topic for mythology and leave it at that. However, I chose to begin this research by asking people about fishing experiences because fishing is a topic that people enjoy talking about, and thus it provides a stimulating basis for discussion, interaction, and study. Talking to Cherokee and non-Cherokee people about fish over the course of this project has resulted in a number of different types of information, ranging from linguistic data, such as discrete names for specific fish, to culturally relevant texts about fish, fishing, cosmology, and the environment. Thus, fishing has proven to be a rich channel through which to gain perspectives on the status of the Cherokee language, the vigor of the Cherokee system of native knowledge, and the history of the relationship between Cherokee people and the local environment.

Methodology

In 1998, when I arrived in Cherokee, North Carolina, initially I was interested in working with the Eastern Band of Cherokee Indians (EBCI) specifically to develop a language revitalization program. I was soon to discover, however, that the EBCI was involved in language planning already, and at that time I could not find a role for myself in the language program. After spending time volunteering with the language program as much as I could, I began to look for another project that would combine my own interests in language revitalization, native knowledge systems, and ethnoecology. During this time I also taught as an adjunct instructor at Western Carolina University and after consulting with WCU archaeologist Dr. Anne Rogers, I realized that there had never been a systematic examination of Cherokee fishing. I conducted some preliminary historical research and then began the process of applying to do the ethnographic portion of the project.

I should mention that the process of application was complicated in that I had to comply with the Institutional Review Board, University of California, Davis, as well as the tribe's own IRB. Unfortunately, the university's process is modeled after those required for medical research, and even with expedited review social scientists were required to guarantee the interviewees, in writing, the confidentiality of their interviews, despite interviewers' beliefs in the preference for clear identification of subjects' knowledge. Each person I interviewed had to sign two forms—a Research Subject's Bill of Rights and a Consent to Participate in a Research Study (Appendixes 1 and 2). Therefore, unless a participant specifically requested that their words be identified in the final project, or unless a participant is a public official speaking about public matters, they remain unidentified. This conundrum points to an important emerging issue with regard to social science research, intellectual property, and collaborative work. Until the social sciences are liberated from the medico-legal model that exists within university review boards, and the nuances of social science research methods are acknowledged by those entities, researchers and the people they interview and work with will continue to be put in an untenable position.

The tribal IRB was overseen by Mr. James Bird, Cultural Resources Department manager and Tribal Historic Preservation officer, at the time of my application. In accordance with the tribal ordinance regulating research in the community, he received my application, reviewed it with the tribe's board, and determined that it was acceptable. Upon his approval, the next step was to have my request considered by the Tribal Council. Mr. Bird had my request placed on the council agenda, and I appeared before it to answer questions about my research. The questions were largely about the intent and value of my research and my plans for the research once it was complete. Once the members were satisfied with my answers, the council voted unanimously to approve my project. From that point my research was overseen by Mr. Bird; he assigned Ms. Myrtle Driver to be my contact person in the Cultural Resources Department, and she mentored me through the research process. She is employed by the EBCI as a Tribal Cultural Traditionalist, and she is a respected elder in the community. She allowed me the privilege of interviewing her about her own fishing experiences and assisted me in finding Cherokee people with extensive fishing knowledge. Understandably, the EBCI Cultural Resources Office and the UC-Davis IRB both required that copies of research materials be presented to participants after the completion of the project. Once I agreed to this condition and the necessary approvals were in place, the ethnographic research could begin in earnest.

Ethnographic interviews on the topic of fishing were conducted with individuals on the Qualla Boundary and the surrounding area from 2001 through the first half of 2002. For the interviews I sought out individuals who were native speakers of Cherokee with extensive fishing knowledge; Cherokee people who are not native speakers but knowledgeable about fishing in the area; Euro-American English speakers with extensive fishing knowledge and families who had lived in the area for several generations; individuals who remembered practicing some of the traditional fishing methods in their lifetimes; and individuals who knew about the contemporary fishing practices in the area.

My primary contact in the community was Mr. Jerry Wolfe, a well-known and respected Cherokee elder, in his late seventies at the time, and an avid fisherman. Whenever I interviewed anyone else about fishing, Mr. Wolfe was always referred to as the local expert. He patiently provided an enormous amount of information about fishing but also about his long and interesting life in the community. He agreed to talk to me about fishing because it is one of his favorite pastimes and something he has engaged in throughout his life.

I also worked with Mr. Charles Taylor, a much younger man (in his early thirties at the time) but a fluent speaker who was raised by his grandparents. Each of his grandparents spoke a different local variety of Cherokee, and therefore Mr. Taylor's knowledge of the language and its use across communities was a definite advantage. He participated in this project to honor and memorialize his grandparents, Simeon Welch Taylor and Beulah Teesateskie Taylor, and he said, "I owe them for the rest of my days for bestowing upon me this unique ability to communicate in the native language, but also for the ancestors who perpetuated this gift of language, throughout the Cherokee legacy of their existence." Interviews were conducted with these and other people from the Cherokee community and the surrounding non-Cherokee community. The interviews were recorded on audiotape or digitally and then transcribed.

When possible, videotapes were also made. Life histories, folktales, and reminiscences provided during these interviews allow for the contextualization of the data such as fish names, cultural practices, and beliefs, but they also provide a clear and personal picture of the changes that have transpired in this community in the last seventy-five years. In this way it is possible, with additional documentary research, to construct an ethnohistory of fishing.

Today, it is difficult to imagine the town of Cherokee as some people remember it. One person I interviewed recalled attending the reservation boarding school because his home in Big Cove was more than a day's walk to town. Today, it is possible to drive that distance in about twenty minutes, depending on seasonal traffic and weather. A younger person recalled as a child splitting wood for his aunt who cooked on a wood-fired stove as recently as the mid-1970s. While reminiscences of life events are an enjoyable avenue for discussion, a major consideration in conducting the ethnographic interviews was that most people alive during the time frame of this research—1999 to 2002—who practiced traditional fishing methods did so in their childhoods, fifty, sixty or more years earlier. Thus the limits of memory and the difficulties of recollection have had a certain effect on this work. However, no one had any difficulty remembering the modern-day methods, and almost everyone I interviewed reported fishing recently with rod and reel.

Fishing expeditions were arranged when possible with people who reported knowledge and experience with traditional methods so that I could observe some of the older fishing practices and some of the modern-day practices as well. An obstacle to practicing the traditional methods, however, is that many of them are now against the law in most locations. Fish poisoning, the use of weirs and traps, and any other restriction of waterways is against state law, and the tribal Department of Fish and Game maintains this regulation in tribal enterprise waters as well. Tribal enterprise waters are those areas of the rivers that are regulated by the tribe itself as a part of the tourist economy and which are regularly stocked with trout as part of its fishery program. There are areas of the rivers on the Qualla Boundary that are outside of the tribal enterprise waters, and in these areas enrolled members may fish as they like. Many of the traditional methods are also physically strenuous and present quite a challenge because in the areas where they are legal, the waters are cold and swift, rocks slippery, and hillsides steep.

Much less physically challenging were directed elicitation sessions, during which respondents were asked the names of specific fish while viewing pictures of different fishes in a field guide or on a laptop computer. Pictures of individual fish were also made into laminated cards so that the person being interviewed could look at them closely and use them for sorting. Audio and sometimes video recordings were made of these sessions. The tapes were transcribed and tables were made of the data. These tables (see Appendixes 3 and 4) show the relationships among scientific names, Cherokee names given by individual native speakers in this study, Cherokee names according to historical documents, and local English vernacular names for fish. Difficulties encountered in employing this method included the variability of the quality of photos of fish (even in identification guides), the variability in the appearance of fishes during and after spawning, the resemblances between closely related species, and the specificity of the locations most people on the Qualla Boundary fish. In very specific locations it is difficult to pin down exactly which fish may be encountered while fishing. For example, field guides often offer generalized maps of habitats and ranges that do not always take into account the differences between such conditions as enterprise vs. non-enterprise waters.

Native speakers and dictionaries were consulted, where possible, regarding the translation and transcription of elicited terms; however, many of the terms elicited for this research do not appear in any existing dictionary because of their specialized nature. In addition to the arcane nature of the material, there are at least two local variants of Cherokee in which individual pronunciation can differ. Thus, the opinions and interpretations of native speakers about particular terms were crucial to understanding the relationships between elicited terms, the fish they represented, and the cultural practices being described. Clearly, the language is a central component of this research.

Literature Review

The research presented in this book may be considered somewhat old-fashioned in its approach; some anthropologists may even see it as neo-Boasian, which I believe is appropriate. Recent reevaluations of anthropological theory (Bashkow 2004, Bunzl 2004, Handler 2004, Orta 2004, and Rosenblatt 2004) have suggested that a revisitation of the initial formulations of American anthropology as expressed by Boas and his early protégées may be warranted.

The rise to prominence of the synchronic ethnographic models set forth by Malinowski, Radcliffe-Brown, and others has resulted in the institutionalization of dichotomies between what has come to be seen since as the "ethnographic self" and the "native other." These dichotomies have circumscribed structures of thought within the discipline of anthropology, and postmodern anthropologists have wrestled with resolving the problem of "othering" that seems to be inherent to colonialist anthropology. "Othering," or privileging the researcher's viewpoint and voice, runs counter to the postmodern project of interrogating and deconstructing positions of power and hegemony because in this construction, the anthropologist is always imbued with the power of description. This perspective has led anthropology to a dead end in the opinion of many anthropologists. The logical extension of the functionalist-structuralist model seems to call ultimately for the demise of anthropology as it has been practiced for the past seventy-five years. However, as Bunzl (2004) points out, American anthropology's founding father, Franz Boas, and postmodernism's primary architect, Michel Foucault, share a focus on "the history of the present . . . developed . . . to interrogate the fetishization of difference" (440). Seen in this light, returning to the early principles of anthropology as set forth by Boas seems a revolutionary act.

Boas had a commonsense approach to the study of cultures and languages: he felt that first we must know them as completely as possible. As a guiding principle he also understood and felt a deep commitment to prove that no variety of human intellect is superior to any other. Rather than seeing anthropological endeavor as documentation of the encounter between self and other, he saw the goal of anthropology as working with members of a particular culture to understand and describe their own particular history of invention and diffusion that led them to their contemporary circumstance. In designing anthropology as a history of the present, Boas believed that one could better perceive the depth of relationships between peoples of different groups and the variety of ways in which a particular group was especially adapted to its environment through culture.

In his tentative early formulations of the relationship between language and culture, Boas laid the foundation for Sapir (1964) and Whorf to construct their hypotheses about the boundaries that language sets for cultural practice. However, Boas himself was extremely hesitant about voicing any ideas about the relationship between language and the mind. He struggled against the prevailing notions of the time that the form of language one spoke was a parameter of intellect and that it limited thought or cultural behavior (Stocking 1974). To popular beliefs about the limits that certain languages place on abstract thought, Boas (1966a) responded: "Thus, it would seem that the obstacles to generalized thought inherent in the form of a language are of minor importance only, and that presumably the language alone would not prevent a people from advancing to more generalized forms of thinking if the general state of their culture should require expression of such thought" (63). As Stocking shows, Boas's early work especially was devoted to presenting language, culture, and race as fluid variables in order to show the commonalities among all human beings. However, as Lucy demonstrates (1992b), in Boas's writings are also the bases of linguistic relativity that later fueled Sapir and Whorf. Boas (1966b) argued, "The general concepts underlying language are entirely unknown to most people. They do not rise into consciousness until the scientific study of grammar begins. Nevertheless, the categories of language compel us to see the world arranged in certain definite conceptual groups which, on account of our lack of knowledge of linguistic processes, are taken as objective categories and which, therefore, impose themselves on the form of our thoughts" (289).

Boas was among the first to realize the diversity and adaptability of native cultures in the United States and Canada, but at the same time his understanding of the processes of culture change and the views of the time prompted a fatalistic orientation in his work. He believed (and often rightly so) that if linguistic data on Native American languages were not gathered, they would be lost forever, and therefore it was the obligation of anthropologists to record everything possible. Today, linguistic anthropologists understand that their ability to work in an indigenous community is solely at the discretion of its members and that the speakers of a language must be the ones to decide whether they want their language to continue. Unlike Boas, J. P. Harrington, and other linguists and ethnographers at the turn of the twentieth century, linguistic anthropologists today, building on the Saussurean model of langue vs. parole and Hockett's (1977) formulation of competence vs. performance, have shown that language is not a set of terms and texts that can be objectified and "saved" separately from the human relationships of which it is a part. Rather language is a dynamic entity, as adaptable and changeable as the culture it expresses.

The work of Boas's student and colleague, Edward Sapir, and his student and colleague, Benjamin Lee Whorf, has been a foundation for virtually all of linguistic anthropology, and their ideas certainly play a large role in this research. However, for this particular project, the specific ideas that Whorf put forth in an article that he wrote in 1940 are especially pertinent. The article, which appeared in the MIT *Technology Review,* is one of the first discussions of the role of linguistics and language in science. He argued, "We cut nature up, organize it into concepts, and ascribe significances as we do largely because we are parties to an agreement to organize it in this way—an agreement that holds throughout our speech community and is codified in the patterns of our language" (Carroll 1956:213). This relativist construction of the nature of science is certainly at the root of most work with native science systems, including my own. Whorf continued with an admonition to scientists that "no individual is free to describe nature with absolute impartiality but is constrained to certain modes of interpretation even while he thinks himself most free" (Carroll 1956:214).

Portions of this research confirm that Whorf's precept that "all observers are not led by the same physical evidence to the same picture of the universe, unless their linguistic backgrounds are similar, or can in some way be calibrated" (Carroll 1956:214) certainly still holds true in the realm of traditional ecological knowledge and our interpretation of that knowledge.

Translation, hermeneutics, and ethnography itself are all subject to the difficulties that humans experience in trying to conceive of one known thing as equal to or at least exemplary of one new thing. Whorf's understanding of the relative nature of the language of science opened the doors for explorations of native science systems, a field of inquiry known at its outset as ethnoscience.

The ethnoscience movement of the 1960s and 1970s has its roots in the work of Whorf and his intellectual offspring (cf. Conklin 1955, 1962; Frake 1961, 1964; Metzger and Williams 1966; Wallace 1965). Most of those working on this topic in the 1960s and 1970s were concerned with cognitive aspects of classification and categorization. The main purpose of this line of inquiry was to understand all of the ways in which humans cognize phenomena in the natural world; in this, it shared a number of ideas and goals with cognitive anthropology and cognitive linguistics. As ethnoscience evolved, for example, the color term work of Berlin and Kay (1969) and Kay and McDaniel (1978), researchers developed methods for comparative study, gathered copious amounts of data, and generated some important ideas about cultural universals. However, this work was ultimately unsatisfactory because, as Lucy (1996) points out, "rather than working from a comparatively induced typology of patterns of language-world relationships, it showed instead the distribution of languages relative to a fixed set of parameters drawn from the Western European scientific tradition" (46). While my own research certainly traces its intellectual genealogy to ethnoscience, especially in terms of topical concerns, the perspective of the work is significantly different. There is a clear relationship between my work and new directions in ethnoecology, as well as general studies of indigenous knowledge systems that seek to understand not the theoretical conceptual models of categorization but indigenous perceptions of the relationships between ecological phenomena and their place in the ontology of a people. In that regard, the research presented here has as a precedent model the applied anthropology done by Richard Stoffle and his colleagues at the University of Arizona's Bureau of Applied Research in Anthropology, particularly their work on the native and nonnative fisheries in Isle Royale, Minnesota.

The analysis, reformulation, and revision of Whorf's work by contemporary scholars have played an important role in the development of my own ideas about the relationships between the ways that people behave, think, and use language. Lucy's clarification and expansion of Whorf's ideas (1992a, 1992b), and especially his exhortations about the methodologies suggested by Whorf's own work (1996), have contributed a greater depth to my understanding of Whorf and greater focus to my investigations. Pointing out what he sees as fallacies in the majority of the research on Whorf's ideas, Lucy (1996) lays an explicitly clear framework about the kinds of questions that must be asked in order to carry Whorf's explorations forward in a meaningful way. By suggesting that researchers reformulate Whorf's ideas as a testable hypothesis, Lucy's work has prompted researchers to find more specific goals in data gathering and analysis. Lucy specifies dimensions of language beyond its referential function to be explored for diversity of thought and experience. In short, Lucy's development of Whorf's ideas has taken research in this arena back to its relativist roots and away from the universalist perspectives that developed through ethnoscientific projects such as the Color Survey.

Silverstein's work (1976) also shows the need to move away from examining only the descriptive aspects of language. He points out that the structural aspects of language that linguists have traditionally focused on are really "unique among the phenomena of culture. Hence, the structural characteristics of language in this traditional view cannot really serve as a model for other aspects of culture, nor can the method of analysis" (12). In response to what he sees as a failing of linguistic anthropology, Silverstein, like Lucy, proposes that language be examined with innovative methods designed to expose different functions, most notably for Silverstein in terms of language ideology. In the chapters that follow I explore the diversity of thought and experience about fishing between Cherokee and English speakers, which can be found on a number of levels, including the referential level but on discursive and expressive levels as well.

As outlined, this research is firmly rooted in anthropological tradition, and there are a number of areas of research into which this project fits nicely as a complementary piece. For example, this research articulates with the extensive work being done on the role of artisanal fishing in the global economy (e.g., Sabella 1980); the work being done on the relationship between traditional ecological knowledge and indigenous resource management (Inglis 1993); and the ongoing anthropological project of comprehending the connections among language, culture, and environment (Maffi 2001; Posey and Slikerveer 1999).

Although eclectic, this project is also integrative. The following chapters show that as a discrete, undocumented semantic domain, Cherokee language about fishing affords a dynamic context in which to (1) develop an ethnohistorical understanding of the function of fishing in the traditional and contemporary Cherokee economy, (2) synthesize an understanding of the maintenance of indigenous ecological knowledge and its adaptation to dramatic local changes, (3) analyze the boundaries of the construction of identity in the complex globalized milieu of heritage/ethnotourism, and (4) examine the parallels and divergences between Cherokee language and English vernacular language about fish. These aspects of Cherokee language and culture also provide avenues through which to document the semantic domain of fishing. In its totality this research provides both documentation—of names, practices, and native scientific knowledge—as well as new insights and perspectives on the processes of language and cultural change.

The Cherokee Language

Prior to the removal of the majority of the Cherokee people from the southeastern United States to Oklahoma in 1838, there were at least three widely spoken dialects of Cherokee, although the southernmost dialect had only one speaker by the time of anthropologist James Mooney's visit in the late 1880s (Mooney 1900a). Two major dialects of the language survive and are spoken by two geographically distinct groups: the Eastern Band of Cherokee Indians, or North Carolina Cherokee, and the Cherokee Nation of Oklahoma, although there are also other organized groups of Cherokees, such as the United Keetoowah Band who share territory with the Cherokee Nation in Oklahoma. The North Carolina Cherokee are, for the most part, descendants of the speakers of the Middle (or Kituwah) dialect, and their present-day dialect is commonly referred to as the Eastern dialect. Most of those who were removed to Oklahoma apparently spoke the Overhill (Otali) dialect, which has come to be known as the Western dialect. The Eastern and Western dialects are still mutually intelligible, with variation lying primarily in the phonology. I have observed conversations between speakers of the two dialects which proceeded with little or no difficulty. There are occasional lexical differences, but these cause only minor confusion. For example, the Oklahoma Cherokee word for tomato is *tamatl,* while in North Carolina the word is *uninekuhisti.*

There is a third dialect in the Snowbird community near Robbinsville, North Carolina, which is called the Cheoan dialect by some. This variant, according to speakers, is closer to the Oklahoma dialect. In my limited comparison of the two North Carolina dialects, I note primarily phonological and stylistic differences that confirm the Snowbird dialect's relation to the Western dialect. One consultant who is familiar with the nuances in both dialects reports a perception that the Cheoan dialect is more proper and uses more complete forms of words and less of what he called slang. The local varieties of Cherokee in North Carolina and Oklahoma are the source of a certain linguistic prescriptivism and purism. Speakers sometimes believe that their local, or even family, variety is the correct variety, and this belief presents some issues for documentation and revitalization efforts.

Mithun (1999) estimates that there are about 11,000 Cherokee speakers,

10,000 in Oklahoma and 1,000 in North Carolina. Both estimates, today, appear to be overstated. The Oklahoma Cherokee recently completed a Comprehensive Language Survey and found that their language was in greater danger of being lost than they had thought. In North Carolina, community members estimate the number of speakers in North Carolina to be between 300 and 500. The Snowbird community has about 300 to 350 members, although perhaps less than half are still speakers of the language. In both North Carolina communities, the number of speakers under the age of fifty is rapidly dwindling; most people in their thirties and younger are monolingual English speakers. There are still a few young people and children raised by their grandparents or by traditional parents who speak the language, but young speakers are increasingly uncommon. Summer 2005 saw the first ever Comprehensive Language Survey in the Cherokee community in North Carolina, which will allow for an accurate assessment of the number of speakers.

Language revitalization has become a serious issue in both Oklahoma and North Carolina. Each community is developing projects designed to immerse children and adults in their language. Recently the Cherokee Tribal Child Care Services center has developed a small infant immersion program, possibly the only infant-age Native American language immersion program in the country. Anecdotal reports show that the babies in the program are already responsive to Cherokee and that as they are acquiring language skills, they seem to be acquiring Cherokee first. The goal is to develop a complete immersion curriculum one to two years ahead of these infants as they enter preschool and elementary school. Adult community members are filling all immersion and Total Physical Response method classes offered by Bo Taylor at the Museum of the Cherokee Indian.

Aside from the infant and adult immersion programs, the day care has a limited language program with preschool-age children being exposed to the language in twenty-minute daily sessions. In the elementary school, programs teaching Cherokee as a second language are tied directly to cultural heritage programs, and the high school offers Cherokee language as an elective. The effectiveness of these programs remains to be evaluated.

The Cherokee language has a unique position in Native American linguistics because it has been documented by both native and nonnative linguists. During the 1810s, Sequoyah, a monolingual Cherokee, devised a writing system for Cherokee with assistance from missionary Samuel Worcester. In the 1820s, after years of observation and experimentation, and several revisions, the syllabary was perfected. Beginning in the 1820s thousands of Cherokee speakers became literate in the Cherokee language through Sequoyah's syllabary, and many documents and newspapers were produced in the syllabary, with 13,980,000 pages printed in the syllabary between 1835 and 1861 (White 1962). The writing system attained wide use in the early part of the twentieth century, and although its use has declined since then, in North Carolina it is still used in several contexts on the Boundary. Recently, Bender (1996, 2002) has shown that use of the syllabary is an important aspect of contemporary Cherokee identity.

While there is much debate over the place of origin of the Cherokee people, by the mid-nineteenth century, scholars (Barton 1797; Gallatin 1836; Pilling 1888), prompted by reports from the people themselves, had shown that the Cherokee language was definitively related to the Iroquoian languages. The other Iroquoian languages, which are located in the northeastern United States and southeastern Canada, include Mohawk, Oneida, Cayuga, Onandaga, and Seneca. In terms of historical linguistics, Cherokee is recognized as the sole member of the southern branch of the Iroquoian family of languages. The Tuscarora language, while spoken by a related group who for some time lived in North Carolina, is most closely related to the Iroquoian languages of the northern branch. Linguistic relatedness is determined through historical reconstructions of words and comparisons of those words that indicate the degree of difference from the original "proto-language." Studies of this sort conducted by Lounsbury (1961) indicate that historically, the Cherokee have been separated from their northern relatives for a longer time than the Tuscarora (Figure 1.1). Like the other Iroquoian languages, Cherokee is a polysynthetic language with thousands of possible inflected forms for each verb. Unlike some of the other Iroquoian languages, in Cherokee the process of noun-incorporation in verb formation is relatively uncommon (Mithun 1999). Noun-incorporation is one of the most remarkable characteristics of polysynthetic languages because entire nouns become affixed into or onto verbs to lend specificity to the depiction of what type of action is taking place.

The Cherokee language has been documented and analyzed by linguists, anthropologists, and others since the early contact era. The earliest works to include lexical items include travelogues by Adair (1775), Castiglioni (1785–87), and Bartram (1793). Later, as attempts were made at classifying the languages of the Americas, Gallatin (1836) led a long list of linguists, including, most recently, Mithun (1999), who showed various aspects of the relationship between Cherokee and the other Iroquoian languages.

In the 1970s the structure and grammar of the language were documented by three scholars. Durbin Feeling and William Pulte's work, the *Cherokee-English Dictionary* (1975), includes an English/Cherokee index and lengthy descriptions of most facets of the language. Duane King's dissertation, *A Grammar and Dictionary of the Cherokee Language* (1975), is also de-

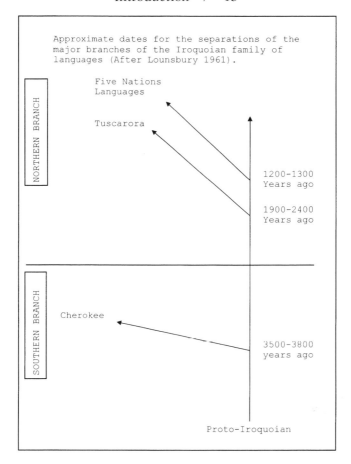

Figure 1.1. Timeline of separation of the Cherokee language from Proto-Iroquoian, based on glottochronological studies conducted by Floyd Lounsbury and reflecting the approximate dates of the separation from other languages in the Iroquian family.

scriptive and shows, in much the same way as Feeling and Pulte's work, the various aspects of the language, with a sizable and inclusive dictionary. William Cook's dissertation, *A Grammar of North Carolina Cherokee* (1979), is based in transformational grammar and is concerned with "the inflectional morphology and syntactic processes of the Cherokee language as spoken on the Qualla Boundary" (1). It stands as the definitive descriptive work on North Carolina Cherokee. Although these three works prevail as important guides to a complex language, in light of the number of remaining speakers, a description of the language with an orientation to pedagogi-

cal processes, further lexical documentation, and updated linguistic scholar-
ship on contemporary Cherokee language use are all pressing needs.

In recent years there have been two additional dissertations written on
different aspects of the Cherokee language. Janine Scancarelli's *Grammatical
Relations and Verb Agreement in Cherokee* (1987) is, like Cook's, largely in-
clined toward linguistic theory and is based on data collected from Cherokee speakers in California, Oklahoma, and North Carolina. More recently
Margaret Bender (1996) examined the social life of the syllabary in *Reading
Culture: The Cherokee Syllabary and the Eastern Cherokees, 1993–1995,* her dissertation, which has recently been published as a book, *Signs of Cherokee
Culture* (2002). Her work looks at literacy, identity, and commodification as
they relate to the Cherokee syllabary.

The EBCI itself has recently undertaken an enormous language documentation project. Federal funding from the Administration for Native
Americans has facilitated the work of tribal employees, particularly Mr.
Eddie Bushyhead, to compile a talking dictionary. The talking dictionary is
a computer database that includes sound recordings of elders pronouncing
words, phrases, and sentences (including variants from local communities),
in addition to written documentation. The talking dictionary is available to
enrolled members, and it usefulness to future generations cannot be over-
estimated.

In constructing my own research, I have considered with some urgency
the number of North Carolina Cherokee speakers remaining; the domains
of the language that have already been documented; and the importance of
the exploration of the relationships among language, culture, environment,
and ethnic identity among the remaining speakers. Accordingly, the following chapters comprise an exploration of each of these topics from the perspective of Cherokee fishing. Chapter 2 reviews Cherokee history in relationship to the environment. Examining the environmental history of the
area reveals human information about how humans organize and use their
perceptions of the ecologies that surround them and allows insight into the
processes that have driven cultural and ideological change. Chapter 3 describes the role of fish in Cherokee subsistence, traditionally and today, and
documents the native knowledge system as it relates to fishing and its complex of methodology, material culture, and culinary practice. The integra-
tion of historical and ethnographic sources in Chapter 3 demonstrates the
value of ethnohistorical perspectives in understanding how subsistence patterns change in relation to changes in the local economy. Chapter 4 examines Cherokee traditional ecological knowledge (TEK) and its modes of
transmission. Traditional ecological knowledge is one means for understanding the construction of a cosmologically based worldview and the related

cultural practices. Chapter 5 explores the connections among tourism, fishing, and contemporary Cherokee identity. Discourse analysis provides a method for understanding how community members delineate themselves from outsiders in the midst of a tourist environment that includes reconstructions of the traditional practice of fishing as an aspect of heritage tourism. Finally, Chapter 6 draws conclusions from the preceding chapters and proposes directions for further research.

Cherokee History and the Changing Environment

Effects on Fish and Fishing

Cherokee people have persevered and adapted their language and culture throughout their complex history, first facing the events of colonization and later the processes of modernization, globalization, and economic development. Each of these agents of change has had significant impact on subsistence practices generally, but the resulting environmental changes have had specific impact on fishing and knowledge about fish.[1] History, including ethnohistory and environmental history, records the changes in Cherokee beliefs and values in relationship to the manipulation of the waters and land of the Qualla Boundary, the homeland of the Eastern Cherokee.

Early contact narratives describe aspects of the environment as it was under the precontact management of the Cherokee people. Unfortunately, the majority of historical accounts do not let us see from the point of view of the Cherokee people what value the land held for them.[2] Therefore we must rely on the perceptions of some of the first Europeans in Cherokee country. Narratives from the De Soto expedition, Adair, and Timberlake show us the perspectives of conquistadores, traders, and diplomats, all of whom took interest in the environments they encountered. Histories of the later colonial period provide a framework for understanding the processes at work in Cherokee communities as they were caught up in the concerns of expanding European cultures and in their own desires for trade and consumption. These competing interests, along with missionization and the turn toward the Christian religion, had a significant impact on the traditional views of the environment. The impact of population loss through epidemic disease and, ultimately, removal was profound.[3]

Ethnohistorical data based on historic documents, other ethnographies, and my own ethnographic interviews allow a glimpse into the lives of Cherokee people from the end of the nineteenth century to the present. Cherokees living today have witnessed a rapid revolution of the local economy from the rural agriculturalism common in the early part of the twentieth century, which required a much more intimate relationship to the local environment, to an ever-increasing participation in the globalized economies of tourism, industry, and business, which are largely removed from the environment.[4] Throughout the history of the contact period, but especially in the last 100 years, threats to the local environment and the survival of its species have been both initiated and mitigated through the activities of its human inhabitants. Ethnohistory permits an evaluation of the Cherokee and non-Cherokee components of those threats and shows us how individuals have adapted and maintained their knowledge of fish and fishing into the 21st century.

This research focuses on the changes in the language, culture, and environment related to aquatic resources that have transpired since contact with Europeans. As the essential context for the linguistic and cultural information in the chapters that follow, here I recount several postcontact periods of accelerated transformation, in which Cherokee people discover ways to adapt and maintain their use of the environment to meet shifting survival imperatives. This focus on historical and ethnohistorical depictions of the environment shows changing values and attitudes toward the waters and lands of Cherokee country.

Perspectives on the Environment from Early Contact Narratives through the Removal

Anthropologists, historians, ecologists, and others now acknowledge that long-held ideas about the environment of North America as a pristine wilderness at the time of European contact critically underestimate the degree to which indigenous peoples were able to understand, control, and manage the natural resources at their disposal. The management of natural resources and the transformation of the environment that have been described since contact times are merely different in scope and method, not in the fact of their existence. Although a reconstruction of precontact ethnoecology must necessarily be left to archaeologists, who can induce conclusions regarding patterns of diet and behavior from the remains of material culture, and to biologists, who can determine the extent to which the environment has been manipulated, it is readily apparent that the pre-European Cherokee had the tools and resources to live well, despite evidence that they had battled outbreaks of epidemic disease even before seeing the first European (Hatley 1995).

While their ultimate geographic origin is still a topic of debate among archaeologists, linguists, and ethnohistorians (e.g., Chafe 1976, Mooney 1900a, Schroedl et al. 1986), at the time of their initial contact with Europeans, Cherokee people claimed control of most of Kentucky, the Appalachian areas of Tennessee and North Carolina, the southwestern corners of Virginia and West Virginia, and adjacent parts of South Carolina, Georgia, and Alabama (Mooney 1900a:14). The Cherokee nation is estimated to have been one of the largest aboriginal groups in eastern North America, with a territory encompassing over 40,000 square miles (Mooney 1900a:14). Although they inhabited a smaller area, the entire area included hunting lands and border zones between the Cherokees and other groups. Thus, in precontact times, Cherokee people had knowledge and use of a much more diverse environment than they do today. They used the area under their control to support an aboriginal population of about 30,000 (Thornton 1990:18).[5] In contrast, the present-day Eastern Band of Cherokee Indians consists of approximately 13,000 enrolled members who live on a reservation of more than 56,000 acres in the ruggedly mountainous region of western North Carolina, adjacent to the Tennessee border, where they live surrounded by people whose ancestors were predominantly Scots-Irish.

Even before physical contact with Europeans, Cherokees both benefited and suffered from the effects of trade with Europeans and enslaved Africans through other Native American middlemen. Waves of disease and material goods passed through the Appalachians from both the Atlantic coast of the Carolinas and the Gulf Coast (Hatley 1995). The entradas of Hernando De Soto in 1540 and Juan Pardo in 1567 brought the first actual contact between Cherokees and Europeans. The people of the Cherokee province met De Soto's army in peace and provided supplies, including corn, mulberries, hundreds of small dogs (for consumption), and Indians to bear burdens (Ranjel 1993:281–283). Thus the Cherokees were able to afford to supply De Soto with their available surplus, which indicates a well-developed ability to manage the production of food and other wealth from their environment even in the face of disease and depopulation.

Over 100 years passed before Europeans came back in any numbers to the Cherokee area. In 1670, expeditions searching for both gold and the almost equally valuable Northwest Passage ventured into the mountains. Instead of finding those valuables, the Europeans engaged with the Cherokees in a deerskin trade that had begun to escalate by the early 1700s. While the Cherokees grew increasingly dependent on their trade relationships with the English (and to a lesser degree the French and Spanish), the emerging deerskin trade reached phenomenal proportions. Agricultural shortages in Europe resulted in leather shortages, which drove a demand for skins that eventually resulted in several hundred thousand deerskins per year leaving the port of Charleston (Braund 1993). There has been an academic controversy over the history of the deerskin trade (or more generally trade in any animal fur or skin) by native peoples of North America. Historians and anthropologists have tried to reconcile the contradiction between interpretations of precontact indigenous beliefs in animism and balance and the wholesale slaughter of animals. Martin (1978) argues that the peoples of Native America were at war with the key animals in their cosmology, because they blamed the animals for inflicting the epidemic diseases that accompanied the arrival of Europeans. Hudson (1982), on the other hand, points out that survival in desperate times far outweighed any religious or environmental belief on the part of the peoples of the Southeast.[6] According to Hudson, the British often dictated that indigenous peoples provide skins or slaves or be taken as slaves themselves. In this context any belief that forbade overhunting was ignored. Krech (1999) argues that the demand among Cherokees and other southeastern groups for European material goods also drove the deerskin trade to reach its fantastic proportions. Krech's argument disallows the possibility that Cherokees ever held an ecologically sustainable view toward the environment and proves that most notions about ecological awareness among Native American groups are the result of romanticized interpretations of their cosmologies. Whether one adopts the interpretation of Martin, Hudson, or Krech, certain facts remain. The arrival of Europeans and the subsequent deerskin trade drastically changed both the way Cherokee people used the environment and the environment itself.

Among the traders who flooded into the Southeast, one, James Adair, lived among the Cherokee and Catawba during the mid-1700s (approximately 1736–43). He wrote *The History of the American Indians* based on his experiences during his years in the Southeast and published it in 1775. He provided an early colonial glimpse of the lands in which the Cherokees had lived for thousands of years: "The Cheerake mountains look very formidable to a stranger, when he is among their valleys, incircled with their prodigious, proud, contending tops; they appear as a great mass of black and blue clouds, interspersed with some rays of light" (Adair 1775:236). The mountains are certainly the most charismatic feature of the Appalachian area, but nearly as impressive are the omnipresent rivers, creeks, streams, and waterfalls. Adair, quite taken by the Cherokee rivers, commented, "Their rivers are generally very shallow, and pleasant to the eye; for the land being high, the waters have a quick descent; they seldom overflow their banks, unless when a heavy rain falls on a deep snow" (228).

Adair found that Cherokee towns are intentionally centered on these beautiful clear rivers: "Their towns are always close to some river, or creek, as there the land is commonly very level and fertile, on account of the frequent washings off the mountains, and the moisture it receives from the waters, that run through their fields. And such a situation enables them to perform the ablutions, connected with their religious worship" (226). This early mention of the role of the rivers in Cherokee belief and religion is evidence that, in the early colonial period, rivers had significance beyond their beauty and usefulness for agriculture. The Cherokee practice of "going to water" at the new moon, where individuals are immersed in the river according specific ritual observances, reflects their long-standing connection to the healing power of the waters and continues to the present day (e.g., Mooney 1900b).[7] Adair spoke of the Cherokees' health and general well-being and related them directly to "plenty of wholesome and pleasant water" (229), but more important for our understanding of the Cherokee perspective on the environment, he asserted, "They are also strongly attached to rivers,—all retaining the opinion of the ancients, that rivers are necessary to constitute a paradise. Nor is it only ornamental, but likewise beneficial to them, on account of purifying themselves, and also for the services of common life,—such as fishing, fowling, and killing of deer, which come in the warm season, to eat the saltish moss and grass, which grow on the rocks, and under the surface of the waters" (227–228). The rivers of the southern Appalachian paradise were central to Cherokee life—subsistence, spirituality, and health all depending on the proximity of Cherokee towns to the rivers. In Adair's writing, we see one of the first descriptions of fishing as part of Cherokee "common life." In describing the common practices of fishing and hunting, Adair shows the Cherokee territory as "rich lands abounding with game and fowl, and the river with fish" (244).

Also finding the rivers full of fish, Henry Timberlake, a British lieutenant who was sent to solidify peace between the British and Cherokee in 1762, traveled what are now the Holston and Tennessee Rivers to the main Cherokee settlement at Chota. As he planned his journey, he asked about the condition of the rivers, and the Cherokees initially "informed [him] that the rivers were, for small craft, navigable quite to their country" (Williams 1927:40). Timberlake decided to travel the river by canoe because he planned to map the water route to Cherokee country in case the Cherokees "should ever give [the British] the trouble of making another campaign against them" (41). The Cherokees strongly warned "that, had the water been high, [he] might from the place [he] then [was] reach their country in six days without any impediment; but as the water was remarkably low, by the dryness of the preceding summer, [he] should meet with many difficulties and dangers" (43). After embarking on the journey, Timberlake and his two-man crew found that they had to portage their wooden canoe for several hours out of each day as they faced alternating waterfalls and shoals, both of which were frequent features of the freezing water. As he recollected his journey, he commented on the natural beauty and abundance of the waters of the Tennessee River. After successfully portaging around an enormous waterfall, he remarked, "The river was here about half a mile broad, and the water falling from one rock to another, for the space of half a mile, had the appearance of steps, in each of which and all about the rocks, the fish were sporting in prodigious quantities, which we might have taken with ease" (52). Timberlake would ultimately learn that the Cherokees knew the river well and regretted the decision that stretched a six-day journey to twenty-two days of "continual fatigues, hardships and anxieties" (57). His experience shows the Cherokee people to be well in control of their environment. He demonstrated that they had navigational and subsistence knowledge[8] of the rivers, knowledge of cultivation of the land[9] and extensive medicinal plant knowledge.

During Timberlake's time, the Cherokees and other native groups in the Southeast were literally caught in the middle of disputes among the three European colonizers, France, Spain, and England. The Cherokees were involved in the French and Indian War and the American Revolution, among other conflicts, and suffered retaliation at the hands of Rutherford and his faction for siding with British in the latter (Hatley 1995). The depopulation during the first half of this brutal century most certainly resulted in the loss of some of those skilled in traditional medicines and knowledgeable of traditional practices. Loss of these conjurors possibly led Cherokee people to doubt their own understanding of the relationships between health and illness and between themselves and the natural world. Adair comments that during a 1738 smallpox epidemic, Cherokee healers tried using the traditional healing practices

and deemed it the best method to sweat their patients, and plunge them into the river,—which was accordingly done. Their rivers being very cold in summer, by reason of the numberless springs, which pour from the hills and mountains—and the pores of their bodies being open to receive the cold, it rushing in through the whole frame, they immediately expired: upon which, all the magi and prophetic tribe broke their old consecrated physicpots, and threw away all the other pretended holy things they had for physical use, imagining they had lost their divine power by being polluted; and shared the common fate of their country (233).

In this single passage lies perhaps the earliest clear description of the consequences of colonization on the traditional beliefs of the Cherokee people.

The Cherokees began to lose faith in their traditional medicine after seeing its ineffectiveness in saving half their number from smallpox. In the context of this research, the last phrase of this passage is particularly salient. The Cherokee people felt that all was lost for themselves and their country. We can see in this passage how they identified themselves with the land on which they lived. In this construction the people and the land "share a common fate" because they are parts of the same whole. The despair over the smallpox epidemic and other epidemic diseases that had swept through the Southeast since the early 16th century must have left at least some of the Cherokee people primed for the efforts of Christian missionaries.

As a result of George Washington's decree that all Indians should become citizens if first converted to Christianity, the Cherokees experienced missionization by various Christian denominations, including the Moravians, Methodists, Presbyterians, and Baptists, beginning in the late 1700s (McLoughlin 1984). All of these denominations are still well represented both on the Qualla Boundary and in the surrounding areas today. The Christian missionaries held a radically different perspective on science, nature, and the rest of the world than did the Cherokee conjurors. McLoughlin points out that "[the Cherokees] saw no difference between science and religion, historical fact and oral legend, man and nature, nature and the supernatural" (198). This difference in perspective, coupled with the fact that Cherokee religion and healing was mostly left to religious specialists who worked in secret, led missionaries to feel justified in their attacks on the old religion. The beliefs that comprised the traditional religion had never needed defense before the missionaries arrived, and the Cherokee priests–conjurors were not prepared to have to explain, debate, or justify what for them was a deeply felt understanding of the way the world functioned.[10] However, in light of the technology, military force, and sheer numbers of non-Indians who were, by this time, pouring into the area, the Cherokees and other southeastern tribes adapted, assimilated, and transformed themselves, at least outwardly, into "civilized tribes" in large part by 1830. Since approximately that point in time, the Cherokee, Creek, Choctaw, Chickasaw, and Seminoles were known as the Five Civilized Tribes. Beneath it all however, there was, and still is, a great deal of syncretism between Christianity and the traditional Cherokee religion (McLoughlin 1984).

For some Cherokees, assimilation to European culture was absolute. A visit to the Vann house in north Georgia reveals that some Cherokees in the pre-Removal period had adopted slavery and plantation owning as part of their culture. The act of becoming a "civilized tribe" was not to be sufficient protection for the Cherokees in the end. Despite the rise of a prominent and wealthy mixed-blood planter class, "civilization" was soon to become a nonissue.[11] Although the removal of some southeastern groups began as early as 1815, the 1829 discovery of gold in north Georgia led whites in the Cherokee area, who had already been agitating for Indian removal, to become especially motivated to take land for themselves. Within ten years they succeeded in having nearly all Cherokees and other southeastern groups relocated. In 1838–39, Jackson's federal government ignored the Supreme Court's ruling and initiated the Cherokee Removal, which forcibly relocated the majority of Cherokee people to Oklahoma. The infamous Trail of Tears resulted in the loss of nearly 4,000 lives through violence, illness, and exposure to the elements. A relatively small group remained in the refuge of the rugged North Carolina mountains, where they persist today as the Eastern Band of Cherokee Indians (Finger 1984).

Ethnohistory: Post-Removal Perspectives on the Environment from Ethnographic and Historical Sources

Today lands belonging to the EBCI comprise in excess of 56,000 acres of federal trust lands in Swain and Jackson Counties, located in extreme western North Carolina, adjacent to the Great Smoky Mountains National Park (Figure 2.1). While some call this land a reservation, that is technically untrue. The land is owned by the EBCI and held in trust for them by the federal government. Most locals refer to the land as the Qualla Boundary or simply the Boundary. The name is said to derive from a Cherokee pronunciation of the name Polly or "Kwali," the name of an elderly Cherokee woman who lived near where the first post office in the area was established (Duncan and Riggs 2003). Most of the Qualla Boundary lies in and around the town of Cherokee. There are several individual communities within and near the Boundary, including Yellowhill, Big Cove, Painttown, Wolftown, Birdtown, Soco, and the 3,200-acre tract (Figure 2.2). The Snowbird community, which lies about fifty miles from Qualla near the town of Robbinsville in Graham County, numbers about 300. There are also Cherokee lands known as Tomotla in Cherokee County, North Carolina, in and around the town of Murphy (Figure 2.1). Although the Qualla Boundary lies in a remote corner of an ancient mountain range, the twentieth century brought sweeping changes to the North Carolina Cherokee.

The events leading up to and following the removal left the North Carolina Cherokees with an anomalous legal status, neither citizens nor wards of the state, neither landowners nor trust holders. William Holland Thomas, a white man and the adopted son of Yonaguska, was a key figure in the establishment of the Cherokees as landholders. He bought tens of thousands of

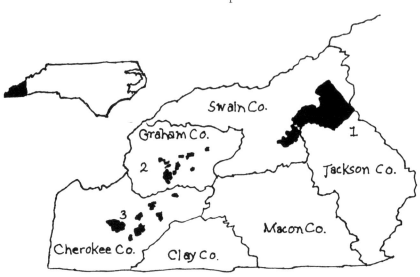

Figure 2.1. Indian lands in western North Carolina: (1) the Qualla Boundary; (2) the Snowbird community; (3) the Tomotla community.

acres of land for them and with them during the 19th century, land that was ultimately legally assigned to the Cherokee. During the Cherokees' struggle to define their legal and sovereign status in the late 19th century, the monies gained by allowing logging on Cherokee lands allowed the tribe both to pay for their land and to pay the taxes on it. In 1881, Chief Nimrod J. Smith asserted the tribe's sovereignty and allowed logging of some walnut trees in Big Cove on the Qualla Boundary. In 1892, after Smith was deposed, his successors sold a large parcel of land, the Cathcart Tract, 33,000-plus acres, for logging as well. By 1900, logging was unchecked in the surrounding areas as northern lumber companies bought up land and clear-cut what is now the Great Smoky Mountains National Park and most of the Cherokee National Forest in Tennessee (Finger 1984). During this time the land was seen by those Cherokees in authority and by those who worked in the timber industry as a means of survival. In certain respects, this period parallels the peak period of the deerskin trade and reflects a reevaluation of ideas about the environment and its role in the survival and adaptation of the Cherokee people. The timber industry provided some of the first wage labor available in the area and began the shift, individual by individual, from agriculture and trade to participation in the cash and wage economy.

By 1901, 85,000 acres in east Tennessee and western North Carolina had been sold to northern timber companies. Logging was in full swing, with

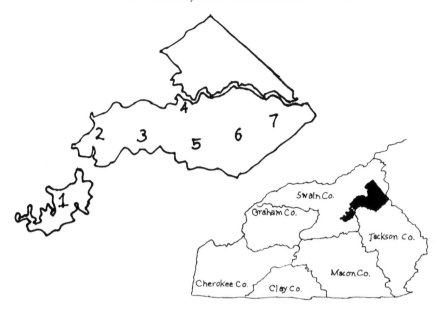

Figure 2.2. Approximate locations of the communities on the Qualla Boundary:
(1) the 3,200-acre tract; (2) Birdtown; (3) Yellowhill; (4) Big Cove; (5) Painttown;
(6) Wolftown; (7) Socco.

timber companies building their own railroads and developing other technologies, such as steam-powered skids, for the exploitation of the awe-inspiring stands of old-growth hardwoods (National Park Service 1981). One person I interviewed reported that his father worked on the railroad for the logging industry in the early 1920s and earned a dollar a day at ten cents an hour, with steel-driving men earning an extra ten cents a day. At this rate, the man saved $150, enough, when paired with a yoke of oxen, to buy the mountain farm that is still owned by the family today. Another consultant reports that his grandfather walked over the mountain from the Nantahala area each week to work in the timber industry for years. The logging industry boomed until about the 1920s, when the limits of the forests became apparent (National Park Service 1981).

In the years following the invention of the automobile, dramatic changes occurred in Western North Carolina, especially on the Qualla Boundary. The tourism that has become the source for most of the economic activities on the Boundary began in earnest with the development of new roads, which were initially built in part to facilitate the travels of Gilded Age tycoons like the Vanderbilts (owners of the Biltmore House and Gardens in nearby Asheville, America's largest private residence) and the Rockefellers (contributors of the money needed to complete the Great Smoky Mountains National Park), who descended upon North Carolina eager to take in its breathtaking beauty, fresh mountain air, and curative hot-spring waters. Soon highway building came to be seen as the cornerstone of the development of western North Carolina, generally, and the Qualla Boundary specifically. As early as the 1920s, highway improvements also facilitated the development of the incipient populist tourist economy in the area. Descriptions from the 1930s show that the area was again being reevaluated in yet another survival context: "The commercial activities of the Cherokees have increased owing to the frequent and numerous contacts with white demand for local products. . . . For agricultural products and Indian artifacts there has arisen a considerable demand, and interest in the dancing and the ball game on the part of whites has led to the formation of Indian companies to travel and give exhibitions of native games and dance in white communities. Qualla itself forms an ideal 'ethno-park'" (Gilbert 1934:214).

Thus began the push for the tourist industry that replaced logging in the cash economy and agriculture as a subsistence base. In conjunction with highway building, the Great Smoky Mountains National Park was conceived of and developed as a conservation area and another economic engine for the economically depressed rural mountain areas. While the fiscal benefit of these developments was touted as reason enough to pursue them, wrangling over land and about the direction taken by the community led to factions, infighting, and deep divisions among members of the Eastern Band (Finger 1991). Despite all that, in the past seventy-five years new roads have been built and existing ones continue to be improved and widened; the Boundary has been made as accessible to tourists as possible.

The 1930s also brought the Great Depression and hard times for the people of the southern Appalachians. People not involved in the tourist industry stayed close to home, engaged in subsistence farming, and relied on the environment for its bounty. At this time the conversations of boys still revolved around whether their corn had been planted. And, according to several people I spoke to, during the lean times of the depression, people fished almost daily to supplement their subsistence.

With the outbreak of World War II, people from Cherokee enlisted in the military. One person I spoke to joined the Navy at seventeen and was on the beaches of Normandy. The violence and chaos of war and the regimented soldier's life were radically different from the life he had known at home in Big Cove. Returning to the relatively quiet life on the Boundary in the 1940s was difficult for some who had become accustomed to regular military pay and had come back seeking regular, wage-based employment. However, new opportunities also arose in the 1940s with rural electrification projects, Tennessee Valley Authority dam-building projects, and Civilian Conservation Corps jobs, which provided wage-based employment for some. These projects precipitated fundamental changes in the ways that Cherokees and non-Cherokees experienced everyday life. Access to electricity, the continuing development of the Blue Ridge Parkway, the formation of the Great Smoky Mountains National Park, and the impoundment of thousands of acres of forest upriver from dams all had momentous local impact.

By the late 1950s, Gulick and his team from the Institute for Research in Social Science at Chapel Hill had found that, as a whole, the Eastern Band was still in transition from a subsistence agriculture economy to a cash economy. Many Cherokees held several jobs throughout the course of the year, with a considerable number dependent on tourism-based employment during the summer months. Participation in the wage economies during the summer months left little time for farming or preserving produce, and winter brought hardship for many as the tourist season wound down with the falling leaves of autumn. Highway conditions were not conducive to extensive winter travel in western North Carolina, and the prosperous mainstream American culture focused on car touring in the summer months as the ideal vacation (Gulick 1960). *Unto These Hills,* the still popular summertime outdoor dramatization of Cherokee history, was developed as a tourist draw during this time, as was the Oconaluftee Village, a historical reenactment of Cherokee life in the late 18th century.

In an effort to develop the local economy, the U.S. Fish and Wildlife Service began stocking fish in the waters of the Qualla Boundary by the 1960s. The tribe incorporated the waterways of the Boundary as a tribal enterprise in the 1970s and took over the program (Maney 2002). In the early 1970s, the tribal government produced a report titled *Cherokee Progress and Challenge,* which provided a snapshot of conditions on the reservation (EBCI 1972). According to the report, at that time the tourist industry was still a major source of employment on the Boundary, although it remained "seasonal and result[ed] in a substantial amount of unemployment during the winter months. Also, in general the wages paid by the tourism industry [were] low and maintain[ed] the Cherokee income level at a point substantially below national averages" (23). At this time unemployment was as low as 1 percent in the summer months and as high as 20 percent in the winter.

In a 1973 epilogue that updated Gulick's study, Neely found that the tourist industry had expanded to include theme parks and a major campground in a formerly remote location on the reservation. These attractions expanded the tourist industry to include more summer employment, but at that time—aside from a relatively small number of manufacturing jobs at tribally owned factories—the tribe still faced obstacles in developing year-round employment (Gulick 1973).

In 1984, the foundation was laid for what is now the most significant aspect of the local economy—the EBCI-initiated tribal gaming. Beginning by purchasing the bingo operation that had been run on the Qualla Boundary under questionable conditions, the Eastern Band took control of gaming once and for all. The 1988 Federal Indian Gaming Regulation Act paved the way for the Eastern Band to continue to develop gaming into a significant portion of their financial sovereignty. In September 1994 the tribe entered into a gaming compact with the State of North Carolina. In 1995 the tribe opened a small temporary casino, and, finally, in 1997, the Eastern Band of Cherokees, in partnership with Harrah's, opened a permanent video gambling casino on the reservation. Since its opening the casino has nearly doubled in size and is packed with gamblers twenty-four hours a day. Its success has expanded the tourist season, which benefits everyone involved in the tourist industry, and provides year-round jobs for some tribal members. The EBCI devotes half its net profits to community improvement projects through the Cherokee Preservation Foundation and has used the other half of the monies gained to increase per capita (or dividend) payments for all. In addition, the tribe and Harrah's are actively recruiting community members interested in being trained as managers or for other upper level jobs in the casino. In 2002, the Eastern Band opened a conference center and luxury hotel connected to the casino in order to expand its interests and opportunities for tribal members. This facility will double in size by the end of 2005, and the tribe is currently pursuing the possibility of live dealer gambling.

Environmental and Linguistic Changes
Related to Fishing since the Late 19th Century

As outlined above, the economic development of the EBCI is closely tied to their relationship with the local environment. Covered in a network of rivers and streams that are manipulated for flood control, electricity production, and recreation, western North Carolina today draws millions of tourists to its waters each year. Any study of the role of fishing in the community's economy must also examine the environmental changes that have had impacts on fishing on the Qualla Boundary. These changes can be demonstrated by the ways in which the environmental changes are reflected in lexical and cultural data and by examining the ways that fishing itself has transformed the environment.

Recreational and subsistence fishing on the Boundary takes place in one of the most biologically diverse regions in the United States. The Great Smoky Mountains National Park and the Qualla Boundary share a border in Swain and Jackson Counties in North Carolina and together provide habitat for over 4,000 species of trees and plants, 40 species of mammals, and 30 species of salamanders (National Park Service 2002). Nearly 50 species of fish live just in the waters of the Qualla Boundary (Mehinnick 1991; Rohde et al. 1994).[12] Historically, logging and dam building have had considerable deleterious effects on the ecosystems of the area. Today local citizens and the federal government are keenly aware of the biological and economic value of the area, and this awareness is reflected in conservation and land management strategies. The National Park Service, U.S. Fish and Wildlife Service, U.S. Forest Service, Tennessee Valley Authority, and Cherokee Fish and Game all work to reverse the damage done in the past, mitigate the present impact of humans on the land, and prevent future ecological disasters. There exists, however, a very delicate balance between environmental conservation and the infrastructure necessary to provide services for local residents and the more than 9 million tourists who annually visit the adjoining Qualla Boundary and Great Smoky Mountains National Park[13] (National Park Service 2002). These next sections explore several human factors in manipulating the environment and how they have had impact on fish in the waters of Cherokee country.

Logging

Logging was a major industry in the late 19th and early 20th centuries, as noted. While logging played a crucial role in establishing the local cash economy and the Cherokees' right to self-determination, it had an even greater impact on the local ecology. Clear-cutting the forests had several related effects, including devastating fires caused by sparks from logging equipment. In the 1920s, there were more than twenty fires, which left the soil unprotected. The bare soil provided perfect conditions for massive flooding, which moved enormous amounts of soil into the rivers. The removal of the overhanging trees also resulted in rivers being constantly exposed to sunlight, which produced a rise in water temperatures. Higher temperatures coupled with the sediment in the water nearly extirpated the beloved mountain brook trout. In fact, today the brookie, or speckled trout, occupies waters only above 3,000 feet, about half of its original range (North Carolina Wildlife Resources Commission n.d.). The brook trout is extremely sensitive to environmental conditions and is considered an index species for environmental health (NPS 1981).

At about the same time as the massive reduction of the mountain brook trout population, rainbow and brown trout were introduced to mitigate the loss of recreational and subsistence fishing (NPS 1981). The rainbow trout, while a favorite sport fish in much of the United States, is a voracious eater and outcompetes the mountain brook trout for subsistence in portions of its native habitat. The brown trout, a European species introduced at some uncertain later date, inhabits the same environment as the rainbow trout. The mountain brook trout is protected in the Great Smoky Mountains National Park and is stocked along with rainbow and brown trout on the Qualla Boundary.

Fradkin's (1990) data, drawn from historical documents that reflected the period between 1700 and 1838, show that during that period, mountain trout were referred to as *adaja*. Fradkin attributes this term to Mooney, so while it is possible to pinpoint this term in time and place, none of the people I interviewed reported it as a name for trout, nor could they identify the word. So either the name has fallen out of use over the last hundred years or perhaps Mooney misunderstood his informant. For this research, however, three specific names for the three different species of trout on the Boundary are reported and shown in the table below. The names in use today are clearly descriptive to some extent, although the name *tsunilodi* for trout does not reflect any particular adjective or descriptor. Names for both of the introduced trout include this word, whereas the name for the native trout does not. The names for brown trout also reflect some of the conflicting ideas about these fish as reported in interviews. The brook trout are often referred to in English as speckled trout, and this name is often also applied to the brown trout because they bear some resemblance to one another.

Dam Building

Western North Carolina is famous for the number of beautiful swift rivers and dynamic waterfalls that flow through and over its mountains. On the Qualla Boundary and in the Great Smoky Mountains National Park, there are hundreds of small branches and creeks that emanate from springs or seeps. Clear, cold water collects into rivulets, branches, and creeks. Naturally, these small streams flow into larger waters which, on the Qualla Boundary, include major named streams such Soco Creek, Raven's Fork, and Bunches Creek. These connect in turn to the Oconaluftee River, which drains to the west into the Tuckaseegee River, as part of the Little Tennessee River drainage system. The Little Tennessee flows into the Tennessee River and, ultimately, into the Gulf of Mexico by way of the Mississippi River. As the waters cascade ever downward to the Gulf, they generate an enormous amount of energy, which is visible, audible, and tangible in the rapids and waterfalls in the area.

Names for species of trout in Cherokee and English

Common name	Local English name	Cherokee name	Gloss
Mountain brook trout	Speckled trout brookie	Unanvtsadv	'speckled'
Rainbow trout	Rainbow trout	tsunilodi	'trout'
Brown trout	Brown trout	Unahnvjvti or Wotike'i tsunilodi	'speckled fish,' literally 'brown trout'

In order to exploit this abundance of natural energy for hydroelectricity and to protect some areas from the flooding caused in part by logging, the Tennessee Valley Authority (Tennessee Valley Authority 2002) began the construction of dams on the rivers of the Tennessee Valley in the 1930s and 1940s. Fontana Dam, the TVA dam closest to the Qualla Boundary, was built across the Little Tennessee River between 1942 and 1944 in order to provide electricity for the World War II effort (TVA 2002). It inundated thousands acres of land, creating Fontana Lake, forcing the relocation of hundreds of families, and changing the local ecology dramatically (Williams 1995).

The mountainous terrain of western North Carolina guarantees that lakes are naturally occurring features only in the lower coastal plain. Reservoirs, such as Fontana Lake, are the impoundments from dams that were built in the last century. Within fifty miles of the Qualla Boundary in western North Carolina, there are five major reservoirs (Fontana, Santeetlah, Nantahala, Hiawassee, and Chatuge) that affect the local waterways. In addition to the major dams and reservoirs, there are a significant number of smaller dams that have also altered the flow of water in the area. The dams were constructed by the TVA or by local, private, or state entities for flood control, hydroelectric plants, recreation, or water supply (Environmental Protection Agency 2002).

The most obvious environmental effect of building dams is that thousands of acres of diverse habitat are inundated and drainage systems are altered in order to meet the needs of humans. The environmental effects for fish are much more specific. Dams form barriers to the migration of fishes and create habitats anomalous to their specific location. In some cases the changes in the environment are reflected in lexical and other differences between people who live and fish on the Qualla Boundary today and those who are reflected in Fradkin's analysis of the period 1700–1838 (Fradkin 1990). In historical documents from that period, Fradkin found mention of one Cherokee name, *jiliya,* for both the sauger (*Stizostedion canadense*) and the walleye (*S. vitreum*), two closely related species in the Percidae family. These particular fish are native to larger bodies of water but migrate up into tributary rivers to spawn. In the colonial and early federal periods, the sauger and walleye would likely have been known to people who fished in the larger rivers, especially during the spawning season. Today people on Qualla do not recognize these fish because they are not present in the local waters of the Qualla Boundary, although they have been found in Fontana Lake (Mehinnick 1991). Dams across the Little Tennessee and Tuckaseegee Rivers limit the migratory range of these fish; thus while they were once recognized and named by Eastern Cherokee speakers, they are neither recognized nor named by Cherokee or English speakers of the Qualla Boundary today.

Highway Building, Pollution, and Acid Rain

The impacts of logging and dam building are obvious and well documented historically. The long-term nature of the impacts of highway construction and pollution render them less immediately apparent. These impacts are documented most specifically in environmental impact studies (e.g., U.S. Geological Survey 2002), but little or no documentation of cultural impact exists, especially with regard to Cherokee culture. Subsistence, a cultural feature, is directly related to changes in the environment.

Perhaps the clearest example of environmental impact related to highway construction and pollution is the fate of the mussels of the southern Appalachians. Two of these, the Southern Appalachian Elktoe Mussel and the Littlewing Pearly Mussel are found in extremely restricted ranges in the southern Appalachians, and both are on the federal and state endangered species lists.

In order to understand how these mollusks came to be endangered, the effects of the industrial age on the waters of western North Carolina must be considered. In the last hundred years, the advent of the automobile, the construction of highways, and the boom and bust of textile and paper factories have all contributed to periods of significant water and air pollution in the southern Appalachians. Interviews with local community members reveal that since the middle of the 20th century, textile and paper mills have played a significant role in the local economy. Both of these industries emit significant amounts of chemical pollution into the waters. The emissions from automobiles and the TVA's three coal-fired power plants in east

Tennessee all contribute to the area's declining air quality. Air pollution becomes acid rain, which pollutes the region's waters and damages trees. Highway construction causes increased siltation in the waters and chemical runoff from the roads. All of these pollutants are detrimental to molluscs, which are bottom dwellers and are often considered environmental health index species.

The decline of mussel populations in the southern Appalachians is an indicator of environmental changes in the area that is part of the pre-Removal Cherokee homeland. Linguistic and archaeological evidence both point to an earlier use and knowledge of mussels among the Cherokee. Archaeological expeditions conducted by M. R. Harrington in the 1920s indicated that the plentiful mussels were relied on by Cherokee people in the Tennessee River drainage, specifically the portion between the Little Tennessee and Hiawassee Rivers near Lenoir City, Tennessee. Harrington (1922) found "thousands of shells of freshwater mussels and of some of the larger river univalves still existing in the river," which to him indicated that these were used as food (216). Mooney (1900a) reports the term *dagvna* for mussel, and its metaphorical counterpart in the identical name for pimple, which as he says is "on account of a fancied resemblance" (308), and the folklore includes references to mussel shells used as tools. In the tale of the Hunter and the Dagwa,[14] a hunter is swallowed by an enormous fish and uses a mussel or *dagvna* shell to cut his way out (Mooney 1900a:320). In addition, Fradkin (1990) also shows the phrase *dagvna utana* (literally large mussel) for oysters, which were probably gained through trade with coastal groups in precontact times. Despite this historical evidence, on the Qualla Boundary today community members assert that there were never mussels in the local waters, and there is no apparent knowledge about their collection or consumption.

Loss of River Cane

Beyond the changes in the fauna in the Qualla riverine environment, there has also been a significant change in species of flora. In particular, river cane, an important element in the making of baskets and blowguns and the source of cane poles for fishing, has been on the decline for several decades, with contemporary shortages primarily affecting basket makers. At one time, river cane was so prevalent along the banks of the rivers in Cherokee country that specific mention is made of its impenetrability in captivity narratives and other descriptions of the environment from early contact times.

The captivity narrative of Joseph Brown (D. King 1977) recounts his experiences living among the Cherokee in the late 1700s. One such experience was to rescue escaped horses that had become trapped on an island in a river swollen by winter storms. Brown and his Cherokee family set out down the river in a canoe to capture the lost horses which "had eaten every sprig of cane they could reach" (213). Brown was made to swim in the freezing water to the island to catch the horses one by one because "the canoe could not be turned in the thick cane" (213).

Although river cane *ihiya* was once thick on most riverbanks, increased development along the rivers, changes in property ownership, and possibly overharvesting have all contributed to its shortage on the Qualla Boundary. The shortage reflects a loss of habitat for the cane and the resultant loss of habitat for fish and other animals that live in the water among its stalks. The conditions that contribute to the shortage of cane also affect the practice of fishing in that the ownership of riverside property by individuals limits access to fishing areas.

Fishing and the Environment

The recreational fishing industry takes advantage of all the other tourist services available, but there is very little alteration of the Qualla environment specifically for fishing. In fact, the mountain brook trout or speckled trout, while a prized catch among local anglers, is highly sensitive to changes in siltation, temperature, and turbidity, so by maintaining waters suitable for those fish, the Cherokee Fish and Game Department is a de facto environmental protection agency.

The tribal fish hatchery and trout ponds are the only physical changes to the waterways managed by the tribe. To ensure that the tribal fish hatchery does no environmental damage, the Environmental Protection Agency monitors its water output for solid waste levels. The water that comes out of the fish raceways goes through settling ponds to allow the fish waste to settle out. The solid waste is removed, dried, and given away to anyone interested as an organic fertilizer for gardens.

Despite the environmental protections afforded by the careful management of the tribal fisheries, local people do report that, over the course of their lifetimes, they have begun to see fewer and fewer of the smaller, native, nongame fishes. Rainbow trout are voracious feeders, and local people report that they consume not the just the insects and other typical native trout food but also the small fry of the native fishes and the smaller native fishes themselves. While this is undoubtedly true to some extent, recent studies have not shown a decrease in the numbers of species represented, and, in fact, new, undocumented species are still found in this area occasionally (Maney 2002).

As fishing pressure increases with the escalation of tourism in this area, there are bound to be escalating environmental issues related to the sheer numbers of people who visit each year. Typical numbers of visitors at Great Smoky Mountains National Park average over 9 million a year, a significant portion of them international visitors. A park survey of about 3,000 respondents in 1996 reflected that 2 percent of those surveyed represented nearly twenty countries—figures that point to the growing global nature of tourism. Spillover of visitors from the park to Cherokee and vice versa is almost inevitable because they are physically adjacent (Littlejohn 1997). While fishing itself appears to be relatively benign, automobile-based tourism certainly contributes to the air pollution and other environmental concerns in the area. Balancing the desires of tourists, the needs of the locals, and the quality of the environment will continue to be a challenge for the Eastern Band.

Summary

This chapter has traced the history of land and water use among people in the Cherokee area from De Soto's time to the present. Throughout this history the perceptions, use, and quality of the environment have changed dramatically. Significant factors contributing to those changes include depopulation and resulting epidemic disease, the deerskin trade, logging, and modernization. The shift from subsistence to a political economy along with the globalization of the tourist industry also contributed the mechanisms for change in the local environment. The following chapters examine the impact of these changes on fishing practices, on fishing knowledge and spiritual beliefs, and on fishing as it relates to the construction of contemporary Cherokee identity.

3
Subsistence, Material Culture, and Fishing Practices

Today, tourists and locals who fish the Boundary waters usually do so in one of two ways—either by using a rod and reel and wading in the rivers or by using a rod and reel from a bass boat in lakes and larger rivers. Traditionally, however, Cherokee people employed a variety of fishing strategies and techniques, a fact that reflected an intimate knowledge of the local aquatic ecosystems and their seasonal cycles. Fishing remains a significant aspect of Cherokee culture—one that has been transformed from a seasonal supplement in precontact times to a profitable adjunct to the tourist industry today. This chapter traces the role of fishing in Cherokee culture from aboriginal times to the present by examining the archaeological, historical, ethnohistorical, linguistic, and ethnographic materials that pertain directly to fishing.

Archaeological sources provide an essential, if somewhat limited, perspective on the role of fish and shellfish in aboriginal Cherokee life and in the early contact period. Cherokee archaeological sites show that while fishing may not have been the central means of subsistence, Cherokee people consumed a considerable amount of fish and shellfish. Ethnographic and linguistic materials show that there are cultural specialization and a proliferation of lexical items related to fishing in Cherokee culture, as well evidence suggesting a certain degree of gender specialization. Specialization related to fishing demonstrates the significance of fishing in the traditional culture.[1] This chapter integrates data on the types of fish, material culture, and fishing practices employed by Cherokee people from precontact times to the present, thus allowing a glimpse through this window into certain aspects of cultural and linguistic change in the Eastern Cherokee community. Throughout the rest of this chapter, mentions of Adair refer to Adair (1775), mentions of Harrington refer to Harrington (1922), and mentions of Timberlake refer to Williams (1927).

Fishing in Precontact Cherokee Society

The archaeological record provides the only information available today about the use of fish as a resource in precontact Cherokee culture, despite the fact that the archaeological recovery of fish bones and other fish remains is made exceptionally difficult by the nature of the remains and the methods used by most archaeologists in general excavation contexts. Fish bones and scales are quite delicate compared to the remains of larger terrestrial fauna. Thus, they decompose relatively quickly and when preserved often pass through the large-gauge, dry screens used in most archaeological projects (Rogers, personal communication). Thus, unless flotation methods are used and a project is particularly focused on their recovery, fish remains are rare. In archaeological records for the Cherokee areas, fish are almost universally overlooked.

Shellfish are more likely to be present in an archaeological context because of their sturdy composition. Thus, most of the faunal records from east Tennessee reflect a considerable number of mussel shells but far fewer identifiable fish remains. In addition, archaeological remains are frequently specific to their location, making it difficult to generalize to other locations. The best archaeological documentation available for Cherokee sites is from the Tennessee River area in Tennessee and the Swannanoa River area in North Carolina, so some variation between their aquatic faunal remains and the aquatic fauna of the Middle Towns (the area of the Qualla Boundary) is to be expected. While the Overhill Cherokees in Tennessee seem to have relied on freshwater mussels to a large extent, those remains tell us little about people in North Carolina. Although these conditions make it difficult to show anything in particular from the archaeological context about the use of individual species among the Cherokee people as a whole, it is evident that a significant amount of fish and shellfish remnants were recorded at Cherokee archaeological sites.

In 1919, the first systematic archaeological expedition of Cherokee sites was conducted by M. R. Harrington (1922) for the Heye Foundation. He focused on the eastern Tennessee River drainage, specifically the portion between the Little Tennessee and Hiawassee Rivers near Lenoir City, Tennessee. Harrington found that "Judging by the numerous fish bones still to be found in the Cherokee refuse heaps on Tennessee River, fishing must have been, to these people, an important means of adding to the food supply" (215). In addition to fish remains, he found "thousands of shells of freshwater mussels and of some of the larger river univalves still existing in the river," which indicated to him that these were used as food (216). In

Harrington's era, archaeological research was a relatively new field and as such was conducted in a less scientific manner than it is today; we have no actual counts of minimum number of individuals (MNI), estimates of biomass, or even identification to taxa of the fish bones. Harrington's report provides a valuable early look at Cherokee archaeological sites that contained fish bones in a better state of preservation than did the more comprehensive projects fifty years later.

Harrington found few artifacts related to fishing, perhaps because many of the material culture items specific to Cherokee fishing were, and still are to some extent, constructed from perishable river cane, vines, and other materials that do not preserve well in archaeological contexts. He did, however, find some artifacts that indicate that fishing was an activity that occupied the Cherokee. He found "a few fishhooks of bone . . . in shape similar to the hooks of metal used today, but barbless; and 'net-sinkers,' which are simply natural pebbles artificially notched at the sides to keep the cord which bound them to the net from slipping off. Such sinkers have been used until modern times by a number of tribes" (215–216). Harrington also comments that there is no evidence to indicate the manner in which the thousands of mollusks were harvested, but he speculates that all one would have needed was a basket in which to place what had been gathered.

In 1939, the TVA formed its original plan to build the Tellico Dam, which was to inundate parts of the Tennessee River and its tributary, the Tellico River. Although the project was postponed for the duration of World War II and for some years afterward, it had been revived by the 1960s. The Chota-Tanasee site, well known through ethnohistorical and ethnographic records as a late precontact and early historic Cherokee center, lay within the area of the projected reservoir. So beginning in 1967 a number of archaeological projects explored the historic Cherokee sites at Chota-Tanasee in east Tennessee.[2] Bogan, Schroedl, and LaValley's analysis of the faunal material from this project reveals that, as could be expected, fish remains are represented but are not well preserved: "The dietary importance of fish is belied by the faunal assemblage, since their remains total 3,097 elements and comprise only 4.74 percent of the total fauna, a distant second to mammal bones in abundance. Furthermore, only 630 elements could be identified to taxa. The disparity between fish and mammal reflects the archaeological preservation of bone and probable differences in the preparation and use of this food source" (477).

Despite the difficulties in interpreting fishing and fish use from the Chota-Tanasee archaeological record, the authors found the remains to be an indicator "that fish contributed an important but seasonal role in the Cherokee diet at Chota-Tanasee" (Schroedl et al. 1986:477). The comment about the differences in preparation and use are crucial to our understanding of the importance of fish in this context. Later in this chapter, I discuss methods of food preparation that reveal some of the reasons for the difficulty in recognizing fish as archaeological remains.

In addition to the data from the Chota-Tanasee site, a Cherokee site at Warren Wilson College (in Swannanoa, North Carolina, about sixty-five miles from the Qualla Boundary) that was excavated by Roy Dickens and his team (1976) yielded fish remains that were analyzed and identified. Fish were represented in the sample in a 1:4 ratio to other faunal remains, and the authors conclude, preliminarily, that a similar ratio existed between the practice of fishing and hunting. However, there is no mention of the differences in the preservation, preparation, or exploitation of fish in comparison to hunting, which would have undoubtedly contributed to their differences in the faunal record. Thus, we must imagine that if 25 percent of the faunal remains were of fish, the actual use of fish was significantly greater. While archaeological evidence of fish is scarce and difficult to evaluate, a number of historical and ethnographic accounts shed light on fishing in Cherokee traditional society.

Fishing from the Colonial Period through the 19th Century

The picture of fish and fishing comes into clearer focus as we move from the archaeological past to the historical period. Firsthand accounts from Adair (1775) and Timberlake (1922), ethnographic accounts of the Cherokee and their neighbors, artifact assemblages, and the linguistic data collected for this project all build upon the archaeological evidence for the importance of fishing in Cherokee culture.

As with the environmental descriptions, two of the earliest sources from the colonial period are Adair and Timberlake. Not only are these sources the earliest, but they appear as the bases for most of the subsequent discussions of Cherokee fishing in the literature. Adair writes specifically of the Cherokee in his descriptions of the countryside and the waterways and gives similar specific treatment to the Choctaw, Chickasaw, and Muskogee. In the last section of his *History,* he rarely identifies specific groups by name, rather providing a wide-ranging discussion of southeastern peoples generally. He devotes a considerable amount of time to his descriptions of fishing in the Southeast, perhaps because he finds that "their manner of rambling through the woods to kill deer, is a very laborious exercise, as they frequently walk twenty-five or thirty miles through rough and smooth grounds, and fasting, before they return back to camp, loaded" (402). Fishing for Adair seems, as it is for many people, an enjoyable pastime. Of the several methods of fishing Adair describes, most are clearly applicable to the Cherokee and have Cherokee language names or descriptions.

Fishing Methods and Tools

Adair describes in detail six fishing methods that he participated in during his years in the Southeast and, based on contemporary practices and other sources (cf. Speck's [1946] description of Catawba hunting and fishing in which he makes reference to Cherokee practices as well), at least three of those can be assumed to have been used by the Cherokee historically. Adair describes shooting fish with bow and arrow or firearms; driving fish into weirs; fish poisoning; harpooning fish with green cane harpoons; "grabbling," or barehanding, for catfish under big rocks; and swimming with nets propped open with green cane splits so that they could be snapped closed when filled. Of these methods, the first was possibly practiced by the Cherokee. The next two are well documented to have been practiced by the Cherokee. The fourth method, harpooning, could easily have also been used by the Cherokee—although the incident he describes is in the Savannah River—because it is well documented that the Cherokees used gigs and spears.

The fifth method, grabbling for catfish, is questionable for use among Cherokee because of possible taboos held against eating catfish. Although there is only one fishing formula recorded in Mooney, it specifically mentions that the fisherman is seeking to catch catfish, although not by grabbling. At the same time, Mooney points out the medicinal role of catfish in the Swimmer manuscript. People that I interviewed who live on the Qualla Boundary have little use for catfish as food, although other suckers are prized. Archaeologically, there were catfish remains recovered at Chota-Tanasee, but it is possible that those remains were used in a ritual or medical context. Chapter 4 discusses questions about the catfish taboo in more detail.

The last method, swimming with nets, is entirely possible for the Cherokees, although the incident Adair describes is specifically attributed to the Chickasaw. Because Adair spoke so generally of the Southeast, each method must be evaluated for the probability of its being used by the Cherokee by examining other independent sources for mention of the method.

Shooting Fish

Adair describes the shooting of fish, either with bullets, gunpowder alone, or bow and arrow. "When they see large fish near the surface of the water, they fire directly upon them, sometimes only with powder, which noise and surprize however so stupifies them, that they instantly turn up their bellies and float a top, when the fisherman secures them. If they shoot at fish not deep in the water, either with an arrow or bullet, they aim at the lower part of the belly, if they are near; and lower, in like manner, according to the distance, which seldom fails of killing" (402–403).

In the 1940s, Speck recorded that the Catawbas (the Cherokees' eastern neighbors and sometime enemies) had, in the lifetimes of his informants, still fished with bow and arrow. Although Cherokees today are certain that their ancestors used to fish with bow and arrow, none of the people I interviewed on the Qualla Boundary had ever done so themselves. Today such practices as a means of subsistence would be out of place in the modern Cherokee community, given the availability and general preference for rod and reel fishing. While it is likely that Adair may have encountered this type of fishing among Cherokees in the mid-18th century, the practice has been out of use for some time.

Stone Weirs

Timberlake found the Cherokee use of stone weirs fascinating: "Building two walls obliquely down the river from either shore, just as they are near joining, a passage is left to a deep well or reservoir; the Indians then scaring the fish down the river, close the mouth of the reservoir with a large bush or bundle made on purpose, and it is no difficult matter to take them with baskets, when enclosed within so small a compass" (69). His description echoed Adair: "The Indians have the art of catching fish in long crails [creels], made with canes and hiccory splinters, tapering to a point. They lay these at a fall of water, where stones are placed in two sloping lines from each bank, till they meet together in the middle of the rapid stream, where the intangled fish are soon drowned" (403).

These stone weirs are still a part of the landscape, although they are no longer used for fishing (Figure 3.1). Rogers (1993) asserts that stone weirs are present throughout the southern Appalachians, including North Carolina, Tennessee, Virginia, and Georgia. She specifically describes three weirs in the Tuckaseegee River in Jackson County, North Carolina. In addition to a physical description similar to Adair's and Timberlake's, she says of these three weirs, "All of these weirs are located in similar topographic situations. Each is in a shallow section of the river, at a depth which would allow unimpeded wading except in time of unusually high water. Banks tend to be low in these sections allowing easy access to the river. In each case there is a large relatively flat terrace present on one or both sides of the river. A prehistoric archaeological site is adjacent to each weir" (48).

Figure 3.1. A stone fish weir in the Tuckaseegee River near Webster, North Carolina. The black arrows indicate the two sides of the weir.

The weirs are found in proximity to significant Cherokee settlements such as Kituwah and Cowee. Rogers points out that as of 1877, any obstruction of the waters was deemed illegal because of efforts to develop the waterways for commercial traffic. Weirs that likely had been in use for hundreds of years were abandoned, but their substantial remnants persist and remain visible in the waters of this area.

Brett Riggs (1999) documents the household items that people lost and requested compensation for during the confusion and destruction of the Removal. His data pertaining to fishing items show that there were "six claims [for] stationary fish weirs in the Hiwassee, Valley, and Nottely rivers," their monetary value thus reflecting the significance of these items. He goes on to speculate that "families probably operated fish weirs on a seasonal basis; large catches may have been distributed around the community" (239–240).

Basket Traps and Fish Baskets

As Adair described, Cherokee people used basket and brush traps in conjunction with fish weirs, a practice they held in common with the Catawba and other southeastern groups. The basket traps were woven of hickory or

Figure 3.2. Early 20th-century photograph showing the Owl family with a fish basket hanging from their front porch. © North Carolina Museum of History, Raleigh.

oak splits and were constructed in such a way that, on one end, the splits
turned inward, creating a funnel-shaped opening guarded by the sharpened
splits; it allowed fish to enter but not exit. On the other end the splits ta-
pered to a point and were closed off to prevent fish from escaping. The
basket traps allowed for the collection of fish at the constriction of the weir,
an extremely widespread practice. As Speck reported, the Catawba also
weighted them to the beds of rivers to catch bottom-feeding suckers,
turtles, and eels. Speck also mentions that Catawba fish traps often have no
opening through which to extract the catch, whereas the trap in the collections of Western Carolina University has loose splits which can be removed
in order to pull out the catch.

It is important to note that basket traps are separate and distinct from fish
baskets, which were common at the turn of the 19th century with several
hanging from the rafters of almost every home's front porch (Hill 1997)
(Figure 3.2). Figure 3.3 illustrates women weaving fish baskets and a number of fish baskets hanging on the porch. The caption with the photo reads,
"These baskets function in the same way a creel does for fly fishing. When

Figure 3.3. Early 20th-century photograph showing women weaving fish baskets. Note the number of baskets hanging from the porch post. The archival record notes that this photo portrays "Aunt Lydia" Sands, the best woman fisher, with her dog "Surlagoochee," on the porch of her home in Cherokee, North Carolina. © North Carolina Museum of History, Raleigh.

fish are caught they are placed in the basket and carried home. In the 19th century fish baskets were commonly constructed of oak, occasionally of river cane, and the baskets were reportedly intentionally constructed to be relatively small, so that no one person could catch too many fish" (Figure 3.4). The small size was also related to the small size of the commonly caught brook trout. Witthoft (n.d.) reports that in the 1950s, "fish baskets are among the strongest baskets made today, and are still turned out in some quantity for local use, but not for the tourist shops . . . because they take more time and trouble to make than an ordinary basket and they bring less on the commercial market. Other basket makers sometimes turn them out on order for their neighbors and they are in common use throughout the reservation today" (106).

Present-day basket weavers construct fish baskets primarily of oak splits,

Figure 3.4. Cherokee fish basket, ca. 1900. © North Carolina Museum of History, Raleigh.

and the baskets are still about 10 inches tall, square-bottomed, with a constricted neck near the top opening to prevent fish from escaping.

Today, most fish baskets are sold as decorative objects. A well-made but plain white oak fish basket at the museum gift shop was priced at $150 in 2002 (Figure 3.5). At the museum gallery there are single-weave river cane baskets that resemble fish baskets for sale to basket collectors, but at $330 these are unlikely to be used for fishing. In contemporary times, weavers also construct utilitarian fish baskets that resemble fly fishing creels complete with leather strap.

Fish Poisoning

Another method that resulted in the capture of a wide variety of fish was fish poisoning or stunning with vegetal poisons. This practice was wide-

Figure 3.5. Fish basket for sale in the gift shop at the Museum of the Cherokee Indian.

spread from the northern portions of South America through the southeast-ern United States (Chapman 1927; Speck 1946). In the Southeast, people would obstruct creeks or rivers and impregnate the standing water with natural poisons such as those found in the hulls and roots of the black wal-nut (*juglans nigra*), the roots of devil's shoestring (*Viburnum spp.*), and horse chestnuts or buckeyes (*Aesculus hippocanastrum*). These poisons, including juglanone in black walnut hulls (which is the same substance that clears a space around black walnut trees in the forest), have a neurotoxic effect on the fish, stunning or inebriating them to the extent that they float to the top of the water and are easily gathered. Speck documented fish poisoning among many of the southeastern groups in detail, specifying which groups used which poisons. He reports that the Cherokee and the Catawba both used black walnut and buckeye, whereas the Chickasaw were known to use devil's shoestring. My own research reveals that contemporary Cherokee people are familiar with both methods.

As Adair described, however, fish poisoned in this manner "prove very wholesome food to us, who frequently use them. By experiments, when they are speedily moved into good water, they revive in a few minutes" (403). Thus, the fish are not in any way damaged by the substances used to stun them and can be gathered and eaten or gathered and revived for use as bait or other purposes later.

In interviews I have found that fish poisoning, long thought to have been out of use since the 19th century, has been practiced on the Qualla Boundary within the last fifty years. I spoke with a woman from Big Cove who described her fishing experiences in great detail. Fish poisoning in this manner was one of her favorite childhood pastimes, which would have been in the late 1940s or early 1950s. She recalled, "What we would do is at the lower end of a branch or of the creek we would dam it up with rocks and, you know, twigs and we'd go way up above and put the walnut hulls in the water. And what it would do is it would just daze the fish so then we'd run back down to where it was dammed up, and by then the fish would start to just float down there. They were knocked out and we'd just pick 'em up and put 'em in our baskets or buckets and the other type of traps I never saw. I've seen them but never used them."

She went on to say that the children of her family would go with her mother or grandmother and make a game of collecting the most fish. From her description it is apparent that fish poisoning survived longer than the use of basket traps, at least among people in her family and community. This same woman later took me on a fish poisoning trip so that I could see how it was done. In her childhood, and even in Adair's account, summer was the appropriate time of year, but we had to go in the fall. Although we had little success catching anything, it was possible to see the method. She spent all morning beating the black walnut hulls with a hammer and placed them all in a commercial bulk corn sack. We dammed up a small pool with things found on the bank, and she shook the hulls out of the large net bag into the creek some distance up the hill above our dam. The water turned black almost immediately, but there were no fish that far up in the stream at that time of year.

Interviews with a younger speaker who was raised by his grandparents showed that there was another method for fish stunning. He reported going with his grandfather and another older man in the summer when the water was low. They spent the morning gathering buckeye leaves, nuts, bark, and roots, all of which are reputed to be most potent during a dry spell. Once the plant material had been gathered in a pillowcase, the older men beat it against the rocks to bruise it and start the toxic juices oozing. The group proceeded to a place in the river where, using the omnipresent stones on the riverbank. they constructed two small weirs, similar to the larger ones described above. At the mouth of each weir the men placed a sack, which was held open and attached to the weir with stones. Then one of the men went some distance upstream with the pillowcase full of buckeye poison, placed

Figure 3.6. James Mooney's photograph of people fishing.

a stone inside it, and threw it into the river. The group sat and talked for about an hour until the young man I interviewed noticed that there were fish in the sacks. They gathered the sacks, got a ride home, and left the fish in the pond behind the house until they revived. The elder men warned the young man not to eat the fish until the next day, presumably to allow the poison to lose its toxicity.

None of the historical accounts attribute the practice of fish poisoning to any particular gender, but these interviews suggest that fish poisoning was practiced differently by men and women. In the two accounts, women and men use different poisons, different strategies, and different collection methods to the same end. A turn-of-the-century photograph taken by Mooney (Figure 3.6) seems to document fish poisoning as practiced by women and children. With the exception of two young men present in the background of the photograph, only women and young children are present. One appears to have a fishing pole and fish basket, the other to hold a stick with which to stir the water. The other individuals in the photograph are women, young boys and girls, or infants. In the photo at least two women have infants in slings. One can imagine from the photo that children were happy to assist and cool themselves off on a hot summer day. The scene allows a glimpse of women engaging in a practice that embodied some of women's gender roles in traditional Cherokee society, including gathering food and caring for children.

Although the Cherokee have a basket specifically constructed to hold fish on fishing trips, the baskets held by the women in the photograph are not the fish basket but sifters—a basket form strongly identified with women (Perdue 1998; Duggan and Riggs 1991). Adair describes a similar scene of women gathering fish in conjunction with handnetting: "During this exercise, the women are fishing ashore with coarse baskets, to catch the fish that escape our nets" (404–405). The use of these baskets suggests that for women, this type of fishing was closely akin to gathering, an activity for which Cherokee women, in earlier times, were renowned (Perdue 1998). If she was stunning fish, a woman could take her children, accomplish her task in a fixed period of time, and depend on a reliable source of food for the table. This was especially important in the summer, when there was little hunting done. When the woman I interviewed about fish poisoning took me out to show me how it worked, she also brought two of her grandchildren so that they might see it done. When I asked her who went along on the fish poisoning trips in her childhood, she said "Well, it would be my mom and my sisters and my brother. And her mother did the same thing. It would be a whole group of them would get together and you know it's just fun 'cause us kids would kind of have a contest going on of who could pick the most fish out of the branch."

In this family there was a tradition of mothers and grandmothers taking their children fish poisoning for food and for diversion. On the other hand, the above description of men poisoning fish indicates methods, materials, and strategies distinct from those used by women. In these two examples there are parallel but different scenarios: where women used walnut materials, men used buckeye; where women made a dam, men made weirs; where women made a contest for the children accompanying them, men used their time to talk. Fish poisoning appears to take on some of the characteristics of gender roles for men and women in traditional Cherokee society.

Men's primary duties in traditional times were hunting, agricultural labor (clearing, planting, and so on), and the conduct of warfare and political relations (Perdue 1998). On the fish poisoning trip, the men constructed and set traps, an activity comparable to hunting. Once the traps were set, they attended to each other and their micropolitical concerns—relating information about community events, discussing the activities of other individuals, and even talking about older times and ways. Other than fish poisoning, men had a number of fishing methods to employ, and many of those methods were similar to hunting, including the magico-religious component.[3] It

Figure 3.7. Jim Tail, Cherokee fisherman. © North Carolina Museum of History.

is apparent from the literature that traditional Cherokee men, and the Euro-American men who described them, viewed hunting and fishing as similar activities. In Figure 3.7, Jim Tail, Cherokee fisherman, is outfitted with the items needed for fishing in the early 1900s.

When I asked an older man about fish poisoning, he asserted that to his knowledge there was no division of duties; however, he said that he had never participated in a fish poisoning trip but mostly fished with a pole with his father after working all day. He did say that he knew of community events when everyone would participate in fish poisoning and have a fish fry. Thus, the interviews appear to indicate that there were various contexts for fish poisoning and that it was much more common in the 20th century than has been supposed. On a smaller scale, family fishing expeditions were coordinated either by women, who took their small children and used gathering techniques, or by men, who used methods more closely akin to hunting and who used the time to discuss political concerns. The circumstances in each case were to provide food for the household.

Witthoft (n.d.) notes that in the Springplace diaries, records from the Moravian mission at Springplace, Georgia, Anna Gambold lists Yucca as both soaproot and fish poison among the Georgia Cherokee. He points out that "as a fish-poison, Yucca is the only plant used in the southeast that depended on an agent other than tannin for its effects, and is more closely related to South American fish poisons than is any other southeastern usage" (230). I have not seen mention of Yucca used in this way in any other account of the Cherokee or other southeastern peoples.

Harpoons, Spears or Gigs, and Dugout Canoes

Harpoons, as technically defined, may or may not have been used by the Cherokee, but similar objects—fish gigs and spears—were certainly used. Harrington reasons that some of the things he labeled bone awls or spear points may have actually been harpoon tips. He speculates that "no harpoons or fish spears were found, unless some of the carefully made awl-like objects of bone, the bases of which are rounded as if for insertion in a handle or a shaft, may have formed part of an implement of this kind" (217). However, what Adair described is hardly what we would think of as harpoons today. He described sharpened green cane "swamp harpoons" that, when thrust into a sturgeon by a fisherman in a canoe, ultimately drag the fish back to the surface because of the buoyancy of the cane. The Cherokee are known to have used similar tools in fishing, including fish gigs or spears and canoes. Mooney (1900a) shows, in the folktale "How the Kingfisher got his Bill," that fish gigs (or spears) were used commonly enough to become part of the folklore.

Riggs (1999) mentions claims for recompense for the value of fish gigs. He found that, in the spoliation claims, "Nineteen claims report a total of 24 fishgigs or fish spears. . . . Multi-pronged gigs and single-pronged spears were used to take fish in shallow waters and were probably employed during spring fish runs when coarse fish congregated in shoals to spawn" (239–240). People have used these types of spears and gigs, or *gatsiohstvdodi,* for hundreds of years, but today in tribal enterprise waters they are illegal.

Dugout canoes were also common among the peoples of the Southeast. Adair, Timberlake, and Speck all mention the use of canoes. As pointed out above, Adair's description of spearfishing for sturgeon specifically mentions fishing from a dugout canoe. Timberlake's entire trip into Cherokee country is either in or carrying a canoe, although his only description of that canoe is that it was "small and very ill made" (42). Later, in describing the

Cherokee and their culture, Timberlake provides a more detailed description of Cherokee canoes and their manufacture. He reports that the canoes "are generally made of pine or poplar from thirty to forty feet long, and about two broad, with flat bottoms and sides, and both ends alike; the Indians hollow them now with the tools they get from Europeans, but formerly did it by fire: they are capable of carrying about fifteen or twenty men, are very light, and can by the Indians, so great is their skill in managing them, be forced up a very strong current" (84–85).

It appears that canoes were still a valuable means of conveyance during the Removal period. Riggs (1999) reports that "twenty-eight households reported losses of dugout canoes (n = 35) valued from $2.00 to $10.00 each," and, as Riggs describes them, these canoes were "probably trough-like vessels hewn from yellow poplar logs" (245), substantially similar to those described by Timberlake.

Speck's (1946) mention of dugout canoes among the Catawba actually describes Cherokee canoes. As he reports, dugout canoes and plank canoes were extremely common throughout the Southeast, with the latter ulti-mately replacing dugout canoes among the Catawba by the time of his visit. The men that Speck worked with were able to reconstruct a dugout canoe based on their own observations and recollections. During my interviews I found that although people do not make or use dugout or plank canoes today, except for demonstration purposes, speakers still know the word for canoe—*tsiyu*.

Grabbling

Adair also mentions "grabbling" for catfish among some unspecified south-eastern peoples, but there is nothing to indicate that the Cherokee practiced this method. Indeed, several people informed me that catfish were not eaten by Cherokee people traditionally and generally not today because, with the exception of the blue catfish, they were considered unclean. In addition, cat-fish are relatively uncommon in the waters of the Qualla Boundary because they generally prefer slow-moving, muddy water. Speck demonstrates that the Catawba consumed catfish but that they used hook and line or, in the more distant past, nets to catch them.

Swimming with Handnets

The last of the methods Adair described was swimming with open nets in hand. Adair was quite taken with the aquatic abilities of most of the peoples he encountered. He wrote, "Except the Choktah, all our Indians, both male and female, above the state of infancy, are in the watery element nearly equal to amphibious animals" (404). From this sweeping statement it can be assumed that the Cherokee were also comfortable or even adept in the water. An interesting contradiction exists, however, when we examine the issue of net use among the Cherokee. Timberlake asserts that the Cherokee did not have nets when he visited them, but Swanton (1979) and others find that statement hard to believe. As mentioned, Harrington found net sinkers, which to him indicated the use of large nets or vine drags in the late aboriginal or early historic period. The use of hand nets was fairly common in the Southeast, and Speck mentions that, at least in the early 20th century, the Catawba had hand nets. Adair's description of this practice is general and could include anyone at its outset. Later, however, he mentioned that he spent the better part of a day engaged in this practice with the Chickasaw, so perhaps this practice was common only among the Chickasaw. It is truly puzzling that Timberlake specifically mentions the absence of nets, when so many others in the Southeast had them and the archaeological evidence points to their existence. No one that I spoke to had ever fished in the method that Adair describes, but one person did report knowledge of "dip nets" or small hand nets. Understandably, however, commercially produced hand nets are now widely available and used in conjunction with fishing rods and reels.

Other Methods

In addition to the methods that Adair described, attention must be paid to other methods Speck reported among the Catawba and other methods mentioned to me. These include fishing with trotlines, bushnetting, seining, and snaring. Of these, I found no specific report of bushnetting in my interviews. This method involved connecting two trees at the tips of the branches. The trees were then stretched across a river with the sawed ends held by a man on either bank. A third man in the river held the bush net down as it was dragged through the water. He would also pluck the catch from the net and throw it out onto the banks. Speck's report sounds similar to Adair's description of the vine drags that were used to drive fish into the stone weirs and basket traps. Adair wrote, "Above such a place, I have known them to fasten a wreath of long grape vines together, to reach across the river, with stones fastened at proper distances to rake the bottom; they will swim a mile with it whooping, and plunging all the way, driving the fish before them" (403). Thus it is likely that bushnetting among the Catawba is a continuation and variation of the widespread southeastern practice of dragging. It is also likely that this practice was common among the Cherokee in earlier times.

Similar in some ways to bushnetting was the practice of seining. The younger speaker I interviewed reported that his grandfather had described this practice to him quite vividly. Apparently, in the middle part of the 20th century, seining was a relatively common practice that involved the construction of nets from old "tow sacks" or loosely woven sacks used to carry a variety of goods. A square frame was constructed of four poles, and the loosely woven material was stretched across it. Six men would proceed to a still, shallow area above a bend in the river. One man would take each corner of the frame and submerge the net in the water, while two would stand in the middle to pull out the catch. One of the men in the middle would go some distance upriver and then move downriver toward the net in the water. As he proceeded, he would make noise, smack the water with tree limbs, poke under the rocks with sticks, and do everything he could to stir all the fish to move toward the net. The men holding the net raised it no more than seven times while singing a specific song. Each time the net was raised the men in the middle pulled the fish out. After seven times the seining was finished, and the men would leave their nets on the bank for use the next time. Anyone who went to the river to seine and saw someone else's net there would leave and go somewhere else.

Much less common than other methods used by the Cherokee, the use of trotlines was reported by one interviewee. Asked to describe a trotline, a fisherman in his seventies recalled

> you have a line, and you have a lot of little short lines with hooks on you know on each one of those string or lines. And you have a weight, you tie it on one side of the river, one end on each side of the river, and in the center you have a weight that drops and that pulls all that down and then those big redhorse (*Moxostoma spp.*) they'll be feeding underneath there. We did that across a dam one time, another fellow and I. I never knew anything about it until he . . . he had a boat and we dropped that line down and it would go deep, and then you'd watch bushes where those lines were tied and when they'd start shaking you knew there was fish on that trotline and that's when you checked your line.

He went on to describe catching several large redhorse in this manner. Although this was not something he practiced frequently, or with his family, clearly this was a method still being practiced into the middle of the 20th century. Speck's description of trotlines among the Catawba portrays similar methods and manners of use.

Although not mentioned in other descriptions of Cherokee fishing, I have found snaring to be a popular method of catching fish. When someone first mentioned snaring to me, I completely misunderstood what the method involved. I imagined something akin to a snare trap for animals—a loop of line or string in the water. Snaring actually involves taking a treble or triple hook, placing it in the water near a bottom-feeding fish, and then pulling up on the line abruptly as soon as the hook is close to the fish. The woman who described fish poisoning also described her grandmother snaring flutterfish (probably the local English name for the spawning phase of the central stoneroller or *campostoma anomalum,* although this has been extremely difficult to resolve with speakers) from the shore in the springtime. She reported, "I can remember my grandmother snaring 'em out and she'd throw her snare out there and she'd sometimes pull up, bring back up, three at a time, they didn't get very big, they looked just like minnows . . . she'd throw that out there in the middle of 'em and jerk it up and have two or three." She described seeing the creeks being completely glutted with the spawning fish, which facilitated the practice of snaring. Another interview with the same man who used the trotline revealed that snaring was often used to catch bottom-feeding fish such as redhorse and hogsuckers (*Hypentelium nigricans*). In August 2002, I witnessed several boys at the Cherokee Talking Trees Children's Trout Derby trying to snare an enormous albino trout they had cornered in a sheltered spot in the Oconaluftee River. The adults who were supervising the event were adamant that snaring was against the rules and reprimanded the boys repeatedly throughout the day. The rules specified that all the children fishing in the tournament had to use methods that were approved for fishing in tribal enterprise waters, and snaring was not.

Hook and Line

Finally, the most common method of fishing, one that continues to flourish today, is the use of hook and line. There has been some debate about whether hook and line fishing was an aboriginal practice or one introduced by Europeans. As mentioned, Harrington found carved, barbless bone hooks in his excavations. In other contexts, bone gorge hooks, such as those on display at the Museum of the Cherokee Indian, attest to the use of this method. However, of all the aboriginal fishing methods described by Adair, there is no mention of hook and line fishing. Whether he neglected to mention hook and line fishing because it was a common European practice and therefore did not interest him, or whether the Cherokees did not use hook and line, is unclear. While hook and line fishing is now well established and has evolved to include mechanical reels, monofilament line, and graphite rods, in earlier times Cherokee people used what was at hand. According to one interviewee, his father used to braid horse tail hairs together to use as fishing line, and Speck (1946) shows the use of corncob reels among the Catawba, a practice that he asserts was common in the area.

The Consumption of Fish Historically and Today

As Schroedl and Bogan point out, ethnographers and archaeologists are interested in different questions. For example, "the ethnographic record provides information on the manner of fish exploitation but seldom mentions the species of fish used" (Schroedl et al. 1986:477). While it is impossible to know the Cherokee names for fishes from precontact times, the Chota-Tanasee materials (from the easternmost portion of Tennessee) show the use of "two species of redhorse and catfish, suckers, sunfish and drum" (ibid.). Similarly, fish identified from the Warren Wilson site (in Black Mountain, North Carolina) included catfish and suckers. In each case, however, the identified fish are a minute portion of the unidentified fish remains recovered. In this section I examine the relationship between historically known names for fish and the names of fish that people use and recognize in the waters of the Qualla Boundary today. The information from this comparison can also be used to shed light on archaeological questions about the species of fish consumed by aboriginal Cherokee.

As mentioned in Chapter 2, the southern Appalachians comprise one of the most biologically diverse areas remaining in the United States. A significant portion of that biological diversity lies in the array of freshwater fishes. As shown in Appendix 4, Swain County, North Carolina, is home to nearly fifty species of fish (Mehinnick 1991). Interviews with fluent speakers reveal that, of those species, seventeen can be identified as species with Cherokee words, with an additional two general terms for fish and minnow. Appendix 3 shows those names tabulated by speaker and includes the common and Cherokee names with glosses and local English vernacular names where available.

In Appendix 3, distinctions between speakers are maintained because they reflect so many diverse sources of information that are valuable in deciphering questions about dialectal and idiosyncratic varieties of Cherokee. The fish names provided by Mr. Jerry Wolfe, elder and avid fisherman (Figure 3.8), are presented in my own phonemic transcription of his pronunciation. The names provided by Charles Taylor, one of few fluent speakers under forty, are in his own transcription and reflect dialectal differences and his use of the syllabary to record what he considers to be the appropriate form. The names provided by Matthew Bradley are data he gathered during his own ethnobotanical research and reflect his phonemic transcription. The names found in Mooney (1900a) and those from King (1975) reflect their

Figure 3.8. Mr. Jerry Wolfe, Cherokee elder and avid fisherman, with his fish basket.

transcriptions and indicate possible dialectal differences among the speakers they interviewed and orthographic conventions of the times.[4]

Analysis of the data collected here is further complicated by the fact that in one case I transcribed orally elicited materials and in another the materials were provided to me on paper in English, in the syllabary, and in what is locally termed phonetic syllables. Charles Taylor, a fluent speaker whose family spoke both the Cheoah and Kituwah dialects, who reads and writes the syllabary, explained to me that from his observation and in his opinion, speakers of the Cheoah (Snowbird) dialect speak more properly. To him this means that they pronounce the whole word, not omitting any syllables or vowels, whereas speakers of the Kituwah dialect speak more rapidly, eliding and omitting syllables. This analysis is similar to that of the speakers with whom Bender (1996) worked. In Bender's case, the analysis of "syllabary pronunciation" indicated a difference between literacy in the syllabary and oral use of the syllabary. In this case the notion of the syllabary pronunciation has been extended to dialectal variation between the North Carolina Cherokee communities. While there is certainly an awareness of the dialectal differences between members of the two communities, at the same time they are still mutually intelligible. Mr. Taylor recalled that as a child he attended a community meeting in Snowbird where, as people sat around a table full of food, the conversation centered on comparing differences in how people said the names of various dishes in the two dialects. The written materials provided by Mr. Taylor and his demonstration of their pronunciation reflect a clear relationship between the characters of the syllabary and the syllables spoken and written phonetically.

Species Consumed

Although the rainbow and brown trout that are present on the Boundary today are exceedingly popular with both tourists and locals, they are fairly recent additions to this area. When people fish for subsistence, they prefer the fish that provide the greatest nutritional value. This includes, most notably, fish during their spawning periods and fatty sucker fish, like redhorse and hogsuckers. Cherokee speakers most commonly report the consumption of several species of minnow (*ajatiya,* or *amakta* as reported by Mooney 1900a), three species of redhorse (*oliga*), and one species of hogsucker (*daloge*), in addition to the three species of trout or *tsunilodi* present. Less commonly reported but still consumed are two species of bass, sunperch, northern pike (from Fontana Lake), and the blue catfish.

Most popular among the minnows are the 'knottyhead' or *ajatiya* (river chub or *Nocomis micropogon*). The 'knottyheads,' 'mumbleheads' *tsunikitsiyvnsti* (central stoneroller or *Campostoma anomalum*), and 'silversides' *unihtaluga* (warpaint shiner or *Notropis coccogenis* and other shiner species) are all part of the catch when using broad-spectrum methods such as fish poisoning, seining, weirs, and dragging. The mumblehead was reported by one speaker to be unclean and inedible, although it is considered a popular fish in the area and others reported eating it. It appears that the names 'mumblehead' and 'flutterfish' both refer to the stoneroller in different phases of the spawning cycle. There was some confusion in sorting out the species referred to here because *Campostoma anomalum* turns red during spawning. Because of their different appearance during different life phases, they are identified by some speakers as different fish. In addition, *Campostoma anomalum* and *Nocomis micropogon* resemble one another to a great degree, especially when they are small, and *Nocomis micropogon* turns red to a much lesser extent during spawning, as well. One speaker reported catching many of the 'flutterfish' or spawning stoneroller, while another reported that the 'mumblehead' or nonspawning stoneroller was an unclean bottom feeder, had an unpleasant smell, and was eaten only if a person was starving.

The knottyhead (*Nocomis micropogon*) is generally favored among the minnows, undoubtedly because of its ability to reach lengths of up to twelve and a half inches, nearly twice the size of the native brook trout. According to one speaker, his father always referred to the knottyhead as the "king of the fish," a loose translation of its Cherokee name *ajatiya* or 'principal fish.' Interviews with speakers for this study clarify a question in the literature regarding the identity of this particular fish. According to Fradkin (1990), Mooney glossed this fish name as 'salmon' in an 1885 manuscript. Although there are not salmon present in this region, Fradkin was unable to identify the actual species Mooney referred to from her documentary research because salmon was a common name among local whites for several types of fish.

Three or possibly four species of redhorse were reported as commonly eaten by people on the Boundary. These include, most regularly, the black redhorse, the golden redhorse, and probably the river redhorse, all of which are referred to as *oliga* in Cherokee. Conversations with Scott Loftis, fisheries biologist of the North Carolina Wildlife Resources Commission, and ichthyologist Robert Jenkins of Roanoke College, who specializes in redhorse, led me to ask speakers whether they recognized the sicklefin redhorse, a species which is only now being described and understood by ichthyologists. Two speakers positively identified the sicklefin redhorse photos provided by Jenkins and Loftis as *junigihtla* or 'wearing a red feather.' This name refers to the elongated red dorsal fin that resembles a red feather.

Catfish (*julisdanali*), while present in the archaeological contexts described above, were not readily named and according to those interviewed are not commonly eaten. There is some confusion over the common names blue catfish (*Ictalurus furcatus*) and channel catfish (*Ictalurus punctatus*). Both are sometimes also known as the blue channel cat. Both are possibly native to the area, although the blue catfish are the less likely candidate for identification in the North Carolina areas because of their preferred habitat and water temperature (Rohde et al. 1994). Photo identification by speakers and habitat preference seem to indicate that the catfish referred to by Mooney and eaten by some Cherokee is probably the channel catfish. However, most catfish, especially those introduced catfish that prefer slow or standing water, were perceived of as unclean and taboo.

Bass, sunperch, pike, and shad are all consumed when available. However, most of these fish exist either in Fontana Lake or in the lower reaches of the rivers where the water is wide and slow. Thus these fish are consumed less commonly but without restriction.

In addition to fish, green crawfish, several species of frogs, and two species of turtles are all considered acceptable to eat. The red crawfish is not consumed but is afforded special respect. Fish avoidance practices and spiritual beliefs are detailed in Chapter 4.

Methods of Preparation

In general, traditional Cherokee women were responsible for the preparation of food and other home management tasks. The preparation of fish was no exception. In more traditional times, larger fish were placed on sticks and barbecued or roasted, as Adair reports. Smaller or bony fish, such as those gathered by fish poisoning, were traditionally stewed until the bones softened and were made into fish soup, as were small frogs. Bony fish, like redhorse and hogsuckers, were all prepared in this way.

Today, sucker fish, such as the redhorse, despite their bony nature, are still prized by many Cherokee for their tasty, fatty meat. In recent times the smaller fish are roasted in the oven on low heat overnight until the bones soften and the fish become crispy. The fish are then either eaten whole or made into soup, sometimes with hominy and beans. As one speaker described, "Naturally, you could . . . the bigger ones is what you fried. But, now, all the smaller ones, and how my mother and grandmother would fix 'em is they would bake them, BROWN, and bake 'em real slow until they got really brown and make a soup from 'em. And you drop these baked fish into boiling water, season with fatback grease and cornbread. Oohh, then you take the soup and pour it over your cornbread. So good." She goes on to say, however, that it has been a long time since she or anyone in her family has cooked fish in this way.

Preparing fish for soup facilitates the disintegration of fish bones and necessitates their consumption, which would make it very difficult to perceive the role of small or bony fish in the diet from archaeological evidence. In addition, many larger fish were probably cleaned streamside and the remains cast back into the water or into the woods, a practice that many anglers continue today.

Summary

This chapter has shown that the Cherokee engaged in a variety of fishing practices aboriginally and historically and continued the use of some well into the 20th century. Over the course of their history, the Cherokee have practiced fish shooting and harpooning and have used weirs, vegetal poisons, fish traps, dugout canoes, seine nets, snare hooks, trotlines, horsehair lines, and most recently rods and reels. The diverse variety of methods of fishing result in the capture of a variety of fish, including three species of trout, three or possibly four species of redhorse, the Northern Hogsucker, an array of minnows, one or possibly two species of catfish, and occasionally various bass and sunperch. As most people have moved toward hook and line fishing, they have also moved toward predominantly catching trout rather than the variety of fish caught via traditional means. While it is apparent from the breadth of the fishing methods available up until the middle of the twentieth century that fish was an important source of nutrition and a widely practiced diversion, fish remains are difficult to evaluate archaeologically because of excavation methods that do not always specialize in their recovery. In addition, traditional methods of preparing fish for consumption obscure the prevalence of its position in the diet.

4

Cherokee Traditional Ecological Knowledge and Fishing

"There's a lot to that; you gotta know the signs"

> Although indigenous knowledge is highly pragmatic and practical, in-
> digenous peoples generally view this knowledge as emanating from a
> spiritual base: all Creation is sacred, the sacred and the secular are in-
> separable, spirituality is the highest form of consciousness and spiritual
> consciousness is the highest form of awareness. In this sense a dimen-
> sion of indigenous knowledge is not *local* knowledge, but knowledge of
> the *universal* as expressed in the local.
>
> —(Posey 2001:386)

In the late spring, riverbanks burst forth in yellow blooms. At the same time
the river teems with brilliant red fish struggling against the current to
spawn. In the Euro-American view these events are unrelated; simply seasonal occurrences that happen to coincide. If, instead, one holds the view
that all living things are connected and have spirits that interact in a realm
outside of our ability to perceive them, these events are related in the same
system, not simple coincidence. In this view a person who understands the
system can read the natural phenomena around him and comprehend relationships based in the spiritual world. Contemporary Western science is si-
lent about issues of cosmology or spirituality because its empirical base will
not allow for the possibility of the unseen or the improbable. In contrast,
traditional ideas about the mythic roles and magical abilities of animals and
plants enliven indigenous knowledge systems with echoes of ancient spirit
beings. While the world is changing rapidly with the forces of globalization
and modernization, the ancient echoes still resound.

Despite the cultural, linguistic, and environmental shifts that have transpired in western North Carolina in the last seventy-five years, members of
the Eastern Band of Cherokee Indians have persevered and maintained,
adapted, and revived their knowledge of local ecosystems and traditional
spiritual beliefs about nature. This chapter examines Cherokee Traditional
Ecological Knowledge (TEK) and describes how that knowledge forms the
basis for Cherokee fishing.

Traditional Ecological Knowledge
and Native Science Systems

As early as the 1940s, Whorf began his considerations of the nature of language, thought, and reality. He pointed out that "the various grand generalizations of the western world such as time, velocity and matter, are not essential to the construction of a consistent picture of the universe. The psychic experiences that we class under these headings are, of course, not destroyed; rather, categories derived from other kinds of experiences take over the rulership of the cosmology and seem to function just as well" (Carroll 1956:216). His understanding that there are alternative categories and that they affect cosmology is at the foundation of many contemporary ideas about ethnoscience and ethnoecology and is central to this study. This section traces the development of these ideas using examples from Cherokee culture for illustration.

Studies of native science systems have changed their focus from examining *ex situ* traditional knowledge, in the form of language databases and classification schemes removed from their context (Berlin and Kay 1969), to developing an understanding of native ethnoecology or, as Hardesty (1977) defines it, "*systems of knowledge* developed by a given culture to classify the objects, activities and events of its universe" (291, emphasis added). The shift in focus, from isolated classification schema to integrated systematic knowledge, allows an exploration of the ways in which members of a community conceive of, perceive, and classify the environmental relationships of which they are a part, as an integral system. Building on the whole-system-oriented ethnoecology model and incorporating values from international indigenous human rights movements of the last decade, scholars have refined the concepts of ethnoecology to concentrate on traditional ecological knowledge, or TEK (Posey 1999).

As one of its foci, the United Nations Environmental Programme (UNEP) has chosen to document Traditional Ecological Knowledge cross-culturally. As a part of the UNEP literature that describes TEK, Berkes (1993) defines it as "a cumulative body of knowledge and beliefs, handed down through generations by cultural transmission, about the relationship of living beings (including humans) with one another and with their environment" (3). While this is a simply stated directive, it presents a complicated undertaking. In order for anthropologists to develop an understanding of a group's traditional ecological knowledge, we must understand not only the names and categories that organize a cognitive system but the whole sociocultural context in which that knowledge is transmitted, maintained, and applied. As a framework for constructing a new understanding of these contexts and processes, Berkes (1993) establishes three sociocultural avenues for the transmission of TEK. First, symbolic meaning is transmitted through oral history, place-names, and explanations of spiritual relationships. There are countless instances of this type of symbolic value in Cherokee culture. For example, the Cherokee name for Murphy, North Carolina, is *tsanusiyi* or *tlanusiyi,* 'place of the leeches,' a name that is rooted in an ancient morality story (discussed in detail below) about events that happened there. Such place-names remind speakers of the spiritual relationships between themselves and the environment and reinforce codes of belief and behavior. Next, a cosmology acts as a conceptualization of the environment. For example, traditional Cherokee cosmology shows a concept of the earth as an island created and shaped by animals. A cosmology with animals as creators of the environment engenders special respect for animals and belief in their power. And, finally, TEK reveals relationships based on reciprocity and obligations toward both community members and other beings, and resource management institutions based on shared knowledge and meaning. This venue for the transmission of TEK is well represented in Cherokee communities with traditional institutions like the *gadugi* or 'organized volunteer labor system' (e.g., Fogelson and Kutsche 1961) and its modern-day descendants, for example, the volunteer ambulance squad in the Snowbird community (cf. Neely 1991). In addition to the obligations community members feel toward one another, Cherokee TEK also reflects the obligations people feel toward other beings and aspects of their ecology. Proscriptions related to particular animals (e.g., red crawfish), beliefs in the necessity of participating in ritual observances of seasonal change (going to water at the new moon), and traditional cultural values that promote conservation or resource management (fish baskets designed to limit the catch) are all part of the Cherokee understanding of their place in their ecology.

Cherokee oral tradition is an especially rich source and an effective vehicle for the transmission of TEK because it is an all-encompassing context for cultural information. By examining particular pieces of the oral tradition in depth, it is possible to understand Berkes's model as it pertains to Cherokee environmental knowledge. First, most of the Cherokee language place-names refer to events in the folklore and provide symbolic meaning for speakers and listeners. As Basso (1984) shows for the Apache, oral history ties the symbolic place-names together with the spiritual relationships between the people or other creatures of that place and the place itself. Thus, by telling folktales about how places came to be named, storytellers allow listeners to feel connected to the place and understand their place in the continuous narrative from which the culture emerges. When a storyteller describes a specific place that the listener knows well—*in that wide, calm pool of water in the river, near the steep, rocky outcrop, just outside of town*—and then relates that place to magical events in the distant past—*a small child was swallowed by a giant leech that rose up from his home in the bottom of the pool*—the listener can easily see the connection between herself and that event. She might think, *"I walked by that spot just last week, I know exactly what he's talking about!"* and the place-name begins to take on a real significance for the listener. The significance, conveyed by the symbolism of the name, contextualizes that place and the listener's relationship to it in a local ecology. Place-names that remind community members of folktales also reinforce the standards for culturally appropriate behavior embedded in the stories. The child in the story had been warned to stay away from this particular spot but played there anyway. Members of the Eastern Cherokee community still tell place-name stories in Cherokee, although more commonly in English, and thus maintain and transmit the symbolic aspect of traditional ecological knowledge despite the shifts in language and culture.

There is also a variety of examples from traditional Cherokee mythology that transmit a cosmological conceptualization of the environment. The description of animals as creators of the earth island is the cosmological basis for understanding relationships among people, animals, and the earth. During the Cherokee creation time, the earth was malleable and changeable. The activities of the animal/creators have an impact on environmental outcomes. A listener can hear the story of how the mountains of western North Carolina were formed—*after the water beetle brought up the mud from the bottom of the water, the vulture flew too close to the land and his wingtips furrowed the earth*—and look around him to see the mountains as a sacred place that has been here since the creation time and see his place in that creation. The award-winning Museum of the Cherokee Indian on the Qualla Boundary has a film and holographic figure that present these ideas to the general public and serve to maintain and transmit TEK.

The idea of reciprocity between beings and the resulting resource management based on shared understanding, the third dimension of TEK transmission, shows up in the Cherokee oral tradition in the hunting and fishing formulae that Mooney (1900a) records.[1] These formulae show hunters and fishermen seeking agreement with the animals they are hunting, which is in keeping with the idea that animals are very much like people and have parallel institutions in their own world. Mooney mentions that animals have their own tribal councils, ballplays, chiefs, townhouses, and the same hereafter. The traditional Cherokee view of animals promotes a relationship based on common mutual ancestors, respect, and reciprocity, which in earlier days showed itself in the ways in which people managed the natural resources.

As an extension and development of the initial formulations of TEK, Nabhan (2001) points out that it is crucial that ethnobiologists and others doing work with native science systems comprehend indigenous views of the interactions between species in an ecology. He shows that "although when one first looks at ethnoecological accounts, some indigenous observations may seem irrational or counterintuitive, they may in fact be linguistically encoded means of validly explaining certain relationships between plants and animals" (148). Nabhan goes on to describe the value of understanding indigenous perceptions of the relationships between plant and animal species and how the names of plant species often reveal something about the behavior of associated animals. In my own research I have found that Cherokee folktales about fish and other aquatic vertebrates often reveal relationships between those animals and other animals or between those animals and the environment itself. The rest of this chapter explores these issues within the context of Cherokee fishing.

Traditional Knowledge and Fishing

As outlined above, Cherokee TEK typically finds its expression in the oral tradition, and TEK about fishing is no exception. Mooney (1900a) points out that "although the Cherokee country abounds in swift-flowing streams well stocked with fish, of which the Indians make free use, there is but little fish lore" (307). While it certainly appears that fish do not play charismatic roles in Cherokee mythology or cosmology, as do rabbits, bear, and deer, for example, the knowledge of fish expressed and maintained in the oral tradition is wide-ranging and demonstrates that the traditional cosmology is at the center of the traditional Cherokee science of the environment. Community members today still recall and tell stories recorded by Mooney long before they were born, and the information conveyed by those stories remains a vital part of local traditional ecological knowledge. In turn, traditional ecological knowledge, specifically understanding the waters, the fish, and the spiritual practices associated with them, is still an essential part of the practice of fishing for many Cherokee people. The rest of this chapter documents the variety of forms of Cherokee traditional ecological knowledge and provides an analysis of some of their common themes.

Traditional Religious Beliefs: A Cosmological Conceptualization of the Environment

The traditional Cherokee worldview emphasizes the interrelatedness and equilibrium of all living things and obliges individuals to understand those relationships in order to survive. As outlined in the preceding section, traditional Cherokee belief holds that people exist in a world created and largely controlled by animal and supernatural spirits, and as Mooney (1900a) points out in that belief system, "there is no essential difference between men and animals" (261). In that world, everything from natural landscapes to disease and medicine is the result of actions taken by the spirit animals or supernatural beings in ancient times.

Mooney documented the myths and practices of the traditional Cherokee people he lived and worked with, and his writings demonstrate the depth of the understanding of the environment among the people he encountered. For example, he reports that the traditional Cherokee view of disease and medicine indicates that humans had become so populous and so problematic for the animals that the animals decided to create disease as a way to punish them. In their tribal council meeting, the various animals all specify what diseases they will visit upon the humans. The fish decide that they will bring dreams of eating putrid fish to people, causing them to stop eating and to waste away. On the other hand, according to Mooney, every plant "has its use if we only knew it, [and they] furnish the remedy to counteract the evil wrought by the revengeful animals" (252). This view indicates an understanding of the balance between population growth and the health and well-being of the animals in the environment.

Another aspect of this cosmological conception of the environment that is still reflected in people's beliefs about the local environment today is the idea of an underworld and an upper world with waterfalls, rivers, and whirlpools acting as the gateways between the two. Water is second only to mountains in prevalence in the local landscape. If we imagine the rivers, streams, and creeks as routes of travel for the creatures of the underworld, as the cosmology holds, then the role that waters play in interpreting the local environment becomes apparent. Waterways are spiritual places, thresholds between worlds, and as such they are also powerful places in the traditional belief system. A conception of the importance of rivers and creeks is essential to one's relationship with the environment in western North Carolina. As mentioned in Chapter 2, Adair's writings showed that "going to water" was in his time a central element of Cherokee healing and medicinal practices. Mooney (1900a, 1900b; Mooney and Olbrechts 1932) reported that "going to water" serves a variety of purposes ranging from traditional prayers for long life and happiness, to traditional postpartum and postmenstrual cleansing, to traditional healing from any number of diseases, to the fortuitous syncretism with Baptist practices, to sporting event preparations. He also documented the traditional Cherokee conviction that water could carry misfortune, disease, and portents of tragedy away to other settlements down the river.

In his description of the "Cherokee River Cult," Mooney (1900b) showed several different aspects of Cherokee beliefs about water. He reports that immersion and bathing in running water is an ancient aspect of Cherokee traditional religious belief, which conceptualizes rivers as part of "the Long Man" and the murmurs and roars of the moving water as a voice communicating messages that only "the initiated" could understand. Mooney also reports that people who were "more religiously disposed" still went at every new moon to be immersed in the water at sunrise while still fasting.

Today, on the Qualla Boundary, people still practice "going to water" at the new moon and at other specified times. Going to water is one activity of the officially sanctioned and supported tribal religious society, the Kituwah Society, which meets at the ceremonial grounds at Kituwah (J. Bird, pers. comm.). There are also other people who practice going to water and its associated observances privately and for specific events such as preparing for the traditional Cherokee ball game.

Taken together, the traditional beliefs about water appear to indicate a conception of the environment that at once incorporates religious belief and medical practice; it includes strongly positive attitudes toward cleanliness, an understanding of the role that water can play in the transmission of illness, and a comprehension of the interconnectedness of all who use the river.

Traditional beliefs about the environment also connected women's fertility with fish. In reporting a portion of the Cherokee origin story, Mooney (1900a) said, "At first there were only a brother and sister until he struck her with a fish and told her to multiply. In seven days a child was born to her and thereafter every seven days another, and they increased very fast until there was a danger that the world could not keep them. Then it was made that a woman should have only one child in a year, and it has been so ever since" (240).

The connection between fish and fertility suggests observation of the spawning abilities of fish and a spiritual awareness of carrying capacity as its basis. If people reproduced as rapidly or as prolifically as fish, overpopulation would quickly become a problem. Water was also connected to fertility; thus, as Perdue reports (1998:23, citing the Payne papers), carrying and handling water were women's jobs.

Taboos and Medicinal Practices Related to Fish: Connections between Fish and People

While fish are not prominent in Cherokee cosmology, they do have some significance in traditional medico-spiritual beliefs about health and well-being and the behaviors thought to guarantee both. This section examines the evidence of fish as an agent in both disease and medicine and as a taboo to prevent disease and misfortune.

Traditional Cherokee cosmology has an explanation of the origins of disease and medicine. However, in practice, traditional Cherokees had theories of disease and medicine that demonstrated the principle of interconnection between living things and events, their belief in transformation and change as aspects of disease and curing, and the conviction that disease and illness are conditions brought on by the acts of others. Disease was conceived of as an intruder in the body which was largely under the influence of a ghost, a spirit, or sometimes a powerful human witch. In order to cure disease, medicine men had to discover the root cause of the illness—usually a violation of taboo or the acts of someone or something against the patient—and address that cause by appealing to creatures in the spirit world that had opposing abilities. As Fogelson (1961) points out, most Cherokee medical beliefs are based on natural analogies. Thus, color symbolism, number symbolism, and similarities in behavior and appearance all inform the discovery of the cause and the cure of illness. In addition to these aspects of traditional medicine, Mooney (1900a) and Mooney and Olbrechts (1932) show that the traditional Cherokee theory of disease anticipated some aspects of the germ theory of disease by conceptualizing certain illnesses as being related to infestations of very small or invisible animals (either insects, worms, or other pests).

Bodily fluids, which, according to Mooney and Olbrechts (1932), included blood, saliva, and gall, were also central to traditional Cherokee concepts of disease. Beliefs relating to bodily fluids primarily reflected the underlying belief in the need to preserve balance—balance between the inside and the outside of the body. Mooney and Olbrechts interpreted the belief in the necessity of balance as a reflection of larger ideas regarding purity and impurity, a value judgment more closely related to their own ideas. Blood, gall, and saliva were all capable of transmigration between the inside and the outside of the body, affecting the balance of inside and outside, and thus were powerful agents in medical and magical practice. For example, menstruating women, who were in a state of imbalance because their menstrual blood was not inside the body where blood should be, were considered to be especially powerful and dangerous and secluded themselves in menstrual huts. Mooney and Olbrechts point out that, among other problems caused by menstrual women, "if she were to wade through a river where a fish trap is set she would spoil the catch" (35). Building on Douglas (1966), Fogelson (1990) reconceptualizes 19th-century European notions of purity and pollution. He provides in contrast a compelling comparison between the power of menstrual blood and the power of the blood of warriors in his discussion of women's roles and power in eighteenth-century Cherokee culture. Both menstruating women and wounded warriors had experienced the migration of blood to the outside of the body, and both were secluded from interactions with others, especially in ritual contexts.

Dreams were also vitally important to traditional ideas of disease, and in the past dreams were seen as agents of disease and misfortune. Specific dreams were correlated with specific events or illnesses. Mooney and Olbrechts (1932) report that by the 1930s dreams were in transition from being thought of literally as causes of disease to being harbingers or omens of illness. This transition away from traditional theories of disease was apparent to a greater degree by the time of Fogelson's fieldwork (1961). He reports the incorporation and reevaluation of terms from Western medicine such as "high pressure blood" (high blood pressure), "goldstones" (gallstones), and "frame" (phlegm) into Cherokee ideas about healing, despite the Cherokees' prevailing distrust of doctors and hospitals. Today, while modern medicine is widely available and people on Qualla tend to use Western medicine, especially for serious illness, there is still widespread knowledge of traditional medicinal plants and their uses, and people often use this knowledge to care for their families in instances of common illness. Kupferer (1966) reported a similarly mixed approach to health care. The maintenance of Cherokee traditional medical knowledge with its gradual incorporation of Western medicine stands in contrast to the patterns of the larger U.S. culture. Whereas many Americans and those in other industrialized nations that practice Western medicine seek to reincorporate "alternative" healing practices into their medical treatment, Cherokee people with traditional medical knowledge turn to Western medicine last.

Fish are mentioned as actors in only two medical formulae in the Swimmer manuscript. Formula 48 is what Olbrechts calls "a beautiful exemplification of the Cherokee disease theories" (243). The formula is for treating fevers of uncertain origin, and in his exegesis Olbrechts explains that the formula shows the fever as being caused by ghost-fish (not harmless real fish) who are jealous of the humans they see from above. The white fish and the black fish in the formula, from the east and west, respectively (the color and cardinal direction symbolism being a characteristic feature of traditional Cherokee medicine), bring heat spirits to blow down upon the people and bring about fever.[2] The cure is achieved by calling the Blue Man of the north to bring the cold and drive out the fever.

In contrast to Formula 48, Formula 68 presents a prayer and cure for a disease resembling diphtheria. The illness is conceived of as insects that live in the water, and the redhorse and his companion the blue catfish are called upon to eat the insects. Fish are seen as healing agents in this formula. The formula, when used with herbal medicine and the avoidance of certain foods that resembled the swellings associated with the disease, was used to clear up thick congestion of the throat passages.

Fish and their terrestrial counterparts, snakes, were included in traditional Cherokee medicine in a number of ways. Dreams of fish were originally thought to cause illness, and then, in later times, to foretell illness. Mooney and Olbrechts (1932) report that, just as mentioned in the origins of disease myth, fish and snakes who have been injured or offended by someone set out to "spoil the saliva" (177). To do so, the fish cause dreams of spirit fish blowing putrid breath on the dreamer until he or she lost all appetite for food and wasted away (15). Saliva, as one of the three bodily fluids, was a significant component in traditional medicine. The relationship between saliva and digestion is recognized in this belief, although their relationship to dreams of fish is not immediately apparent.

A recent study (Malainey et al. 2001), however, indicates that peoples who eat lean red meat regularly, as in their example of the hunting-based economies of the northern Plains region, often have digestive difficulty when incorporating fish into the diet seasonally or when economic conditions change. The digestive difficulties often lead to fish avoidance or prohibition. The relationship between fish and indigestion in the Cherokee traditional belief system possibly reflects digestive difficulties in adjusting to the seasonal nature of fishing and hunting in traditional Cherokee culture. As mentioned in Chapter 2, there has been extensive debate among archaeologists, linguists, and ethnohistorians about the geographic origins of the Cherokee people. Thus, the beliefs about fish and indigestion could possibly be quite old and reflective of a time when the Cherokee may have lived elsewhere and were more reliant on buffalo, elk, deer, and other meats. Taboos relating to digestion and illness regarding the consumption of fish make sense in either scenario. Future research on this question should include the investigation of historical linguistic data and cultural practices relating to fish among southeastern groups and among northern Iroquoian groups. While historical linguistic studies can show when and from where words for different species of fish entered the language, comparing Cherokee taboos or avoidance practices with those of other culture groups could also show patterns that provide insight into migration and settlement patterns.

Some of the earliest documentary materials that relate information about traditional taboos are the pages of the Springplace diaries, an account of the Moravian mission in Springplace, Georgia, from the early 1800s. The Springplace diaries, archived at the Moravian archives in Winston-Salem,

North Carolina, provide fascinating information about daily life at the mission and among the Cherokee. One entry, from September 20, 1814, indicates that a student visited the missionaries and described the medical treatment he had received from a traditional doctor. The missionaries recorded his narrative about how he was scratched "with a saw-shaped lower jaw of a fish in the waters here, with which long stripes are pulled through the skin at small distances, so that it then looks completely bloody. The Indians put great stock in this, and also use it as a method of punishing their children, to make them better. Our children often carry this out on each other, as they say to make themselves nimble. Dawzizi also said the 'Doctor' drew a little horn of blood from his forehead and back of his head, which provided him the desired effect against headaches" (1814:46). This medicinal use of a fish jaw is also reflected in the archaeological data analyzed by Bogan. In the materials from Chota-Tanasee, he found that "the longnose gar is represented by six fragments, including two dentary pieces, one of which has the distal end cut off. This suggests that the gar fish elements may have been modified for practical uses such as scrapers and fish hooks" (Schroedl et al. 1986:477). The Springplace diaries provide us with a clear picture of the uses of gar teeth. Rather than scrapers or fish hooks, it is likely that the modified gar dentary pieces were used for scratching in ceremonial or medicinal contexts. According to Fradkin (1990), the Butrick papers report that gar are considered taboo and must not be eaten. The role of gar in traditional culture appears to be only as a tool in ceremonial contexts. Today gar are uncommon in the area of the Qualla Boundary because they prefer lakes, pools, and weedy areas that are not part of the natural landscape of free-flowing mountain streams (Rohde et al. 1994). None of the people I interviewed reported knowing this fish from local waters, although most recognized it as being present in Fontana Lake, an observation confirmed by Mehinnick (1991).

Mooney records the practice of scratching with a "bone-tooth comb" among the North Carolina Cherokee (1900a:230). While the practice of scratching is still reported today in the Eastern Cherokee community, especially in preparation for the ball game, the practice is performed with other types of implements such as thorns or metal implements. Thus, it seems likely that in places like east Tennessee and north Georgia where gar are more common, they were more commonly used in the scratching procedure.

Mooney (1900a) and Mooney and Olbrechts document taboos against eating certain fish that pertain to individuals in particular conditions. For instance, speckled trout were feared to cause black marks or an uneven complexion in babies and possibly excessive bleeding during delivery (Mooney and Olbrechts 1932:120), and no fish were to be consumed postpartum because of a belief that the cold-blooded nature of the fish would cause clotting and prevent the expulsion of the postpartum blood. Hogsuckers were taboo to ballplayers because it was believed that the sluggishness of the fish would translate to the players' abilities (Mooney 1900a).

On the other hand, ballplayers were encouraged to rub themselves with eel skins to make themselves slippery, and women tied their hair with eel skins to make it long and sleek (Mooney 1900a). Apparently, however, eels were not thought to be consumable fish. The Springplace diaries show that on "May 11th. One of our pupils brought us a large eel he had caught. The Indians here do not eat eel, but they do eat the flesh of the rattlesnake" (1825:11). Fradkin (1990) also reports that Butrick includes eels among the fish not to be eaten by anyone, with one exception: the oil fried out of eel skins was given to those with rheumatism to ease their stiffness (Mooney and Olbrechts 1932). The actual fish referred to in each of these accounts is probably the mountain brook lamprey, since true eels do not make it into the mountains from the Atlantic Coast (Rohde et al. 1994). However, people recognize and identify "eels" easily today, although no one reports eating them. No one I interviewed reported any medicinal use for eels today, and they are described by most people as being uncommon in the area.

There were a number of other fish taboos reported by Mooney and Olbrechts: the prohibition of all fish to anyone with diarrhea because the loose nature of fish feces gives the appearance of diarrhea; the prohibition of the sun perch *agola* and buffalo fish *gasudv* to those with rheumatism because the hump-backed appearance of these fish seemed to indicate that they suffered from rheumatism themselves; the prohibition of the central stoneroller *tsvnigitsiyvnsti* for a number of conditions but specifically for certain serious forms of indigestion because it decays rapidly. In the interviews for this research, one person did report a belief that the central stoneroller was not good to eat because it smelled bad and should be consumed only if one was starving, while another reported catching them in great numbers during the spawning season, which may reflect its reevaluation as a different fish because of its apparent transformation during the spawning season. The people interviewed report no knowledge of the buffalo fish, and indeed it is not recorded in the area.

Any of these fish mentioned could correlate with the fish mentioned as taboo in the Springplace diaries on July 16, 1827. From that entry we see that "Josua brought us a large tasty fish . . . out of superstition, the Indians do not eat this fish. They say their ["Melonen und Gurken" or "Gnoken" ???] would get messed up" (1827:15). The questions in square brackets were provided by the translator of the diary, probably owing to a combination of difficulty in reading the author's handwriting and making sense of what this meant. A search of standard German references reveals that 'gnoken' is not a word in German. 'Melonen and gurken' translates as melons and cucumbers so it appears that the taboo was to protect gardening.

Additional research at the American Philosophical Society Archives has provided some supplementary information about this point. A manuscript in its collection, prepared by John Witthoft in 1953, reports that Cherokees must "Either keep away from the plant [May apple] or raise no melons, pumpkins, cucumbers, squash, or gourds (beans are exempt from this danger). I have never been able to learn of any explanation or rationalization for this belief, *which also holds for a salamander, the 'water dog,' which must not be eaten during the growing season of vine crops for the same reason*" (39, emphasis added). This would seem to indicate that Moravians' account of the taboo against eating the "large, tasty fish" might have been against eating the salamander. This taboo does appear especially related to growing a certain class of vine-grown fruits and vegetables. Witthoft does go on to note that with the exception of the aforementioned taboo, "small fish, frogs (called toads in Reservation English), and Necturis, the large river salimander (called 'water-dog'; a term used throughout the mountains and Piedmont from central Pennsylvania south) were often boiled into soup" (159).

Fradkin (1990) reports that passages in the Butrick papers assert a prohibition against the consumption of catfish, and, while I found no report of an actual taboo, everyone I interviewed professes a belief that the majority of catfish are unclean and inedible. The one exception is what is known locally as the blue catfish, or commonly as the channel catfish (*Ictalurus punctatus*), as identified by photograph. This is the blue catfish of the fishing formula and the medicinal formula for diphtheria. The blue catfish is considered edible; however, it must be skinned properly. The fish commonly known as the blue catfish (*Ictalurus furcatus*) in the ichthyology literature is not reported in the Cherokee area (Mehinnick 1991). It appears that most people in the area do not eat any species of catfish regularly.

The last taboo found in the literature and still practiced today is the prohibition against eating red crawfish. There are two types of crawfish or crayfish that appear in Cherokee mythology—the red and the green. The red crayfish has a role in one of the creation stories. According to Mooney (1900a), after the earth had been formed and the land was dry and the spirit-animals came down from the sky, the earth was dark. After they obtained the sun, they initially set it in its track just overhead. However, it was too close to the earth "and Tsiskagili, the Red Crawfish, had his shell scorched a bright red, so that his meat was spoiled; and the Cherokee do not eat it" (239). Laura H. King (1977), an anthropologist and enrolled member of the

Eastern Band, collected this story, in a slightly altered form, from Snowbird resident Lula "Nicey" Welch. In Ms. Welch's version the green and the red crayfish are walking along when they encounter "Skina," who tries to entice them to follow him. Only one crayfish follows, and,

> As he kept getting closer and closer to the land of fire, the temperature continued to gradually rise. As a result, the crayfish did not notice that his body was turning red from the heat. The other crayfish following some distance behind noticed the change in his friend's shell. Instinctively he began retreating backwards, in the motion in which crayfish have moved ever since that day. When he reached the water, he was so frightened, that he jumped into the water and from that day forward, Tsi-stv-na (green crayfish) continues to dwell in that habitat.
>
> The red scorched crayfish, Tsi-sko-ki-li, when he realized his shell was burning, dug a hole in the soft mud to cool off. The red crayfish has ever since lived in the mud. Its meat was spoiled by the heat and the Cherokees do not eat it. However, water emerging from the hole, where the red crayfish lives, is revered for its medicinal properties and is used today for curing an individual who is hard of hearing. (King 1977:246)

In her commentary, King points out the Judeo-Christian influence in the story which is apparent in the name "Skina," what Cherokee people today call the devil. However, the medicinal use of the crawfish hole water is not recorded elsewhere. In interviews for this research, people report that the red crawfish is still not consumed. One speaker said simply that one must leave it alone and "give it the proper respect," and another reported that the meat does not taste good; it "tastes like mud."

Fishing Charms: TEK in Microcosm

Fishing and hunting formulas or charms were used by traditional conjurors to influence the inhabitants of the natural world to provide for the success of hunters or fishermen. Mooney (1900a) reported that, in his day, one could buy a fishing charm from a conjuror but predicted, even in the late 1890s, that these charms would soon fade from use. He also attests to their presence in the formula books of local conjurors. In preparing this research I requested copies of a manuscript listed as "Hunting and Fishing formulae" from the National Anthropological Archives in the hope that it would hold a collection of these formulae. When I read through the materials, however, it became apparent that the manuscripts were, as promised in the catalogue, "incomplete."[3] It is unclear whether Mooney was simply making notes to himself for future projects that were never finished or whether these materials were lost. Some are apparently included in the "Sacred Formulas" portion of the Mooney text, but it is not clear what happened to the rest.

Preliminary examination of the materials from the Mooney archival materials available has revealed no overt references to fish; however, the archaic and metaphorical nature of the language in the formulae may obscure the true nature of the words. Aside from the few formulae included in these materials, there are what appear to be line-by-line translations of letters and other documents that bear no relation to the rest of the materials. In addition, most of the materials are handwritten by Mooney and the original owners in the syllabary, making it exceedingly difficult to decipher them (Mooney n.d.). Future research will include working with native Cherokee speakers who are literate in the syllabary to decipher the materials that are present and to determine which, if any, of them are fishing formulae. Mooney (1900a) shares one fishing formula from the Swimmer manuscript:

> This Is for Catching Large Fish
>
> Listen! Now you settlements have drawn near to hearken. Where you have gathered in the foam you are moving about as one. You Blue Cat and the others, I have come to offer you freely the white food. Let the paths from every direction recognize each other. Our spittle shall be in agreement. Let them (your and my spittle) be together as we go about. They (the fish) have become a prey and there shall be no loneliness. Your spittle has become agreeable. I am called Swimmer. Yu! (374–375)

Mooney's explanation and annotations of the metaphors in the formula provide a nutshell description of the traditional ecological knowledge of that era. The formula and its instructions for use show the conceptualization of the world of the fish, the relationship between a particular plant and the act of fishing, the necessity for agreement and reciprocity between the fisherman and fish, and the symbolic value of words that even in Mooney's era were so archaic they had no literal meaning.

In the explanation of the formula, Mooney shows that the words are addressed directly to the fish, which are portrayed as having underwater settlements, traveling regular paths through the water, and having the desire to gather together as if to greet old friends. Reflected in this conceptualization is the understanding, through observation, that individual species of fish do tend to prefer particular habitats, do have regular migratory patterns, and do come together in schools or groups. The metaphors of the formula describe all of these characteristics in human terms, once again demonstrating the essential unity of humans and other creatures in the cosmology.

Mooney reports that Swimmer's manuscript, from which the formula is taken, instructs that the fisherman must first obtain the root of the Venus Flytrap, chew a small piece, and spit this on the bait and hook. People interviewed for this research report the practice of chewing the root of the trout lily (*Erythroni americanum*) and spitting it on the hook, at least in memory, but the annotation supplied by Mooney indicates that the Venus Flytrap was used with this formula because of it symbolic holding power. Fish were believed to be held on the hook by the Venus Flytrap roots just as insects were caught in the traps themselves. The Venus Flytrap is native only to the coastal bog areas of North and South Carolina, so they must have been obtained through trade or perhaps there was a misunderstanding between Mooney and Swimmer as to the name and nature of the plant. If these plants were obtained through trade, then the knowledge of their use must also have been obtained from tribes farther east.

In the formula, the accord of the fisherman and the fish is so great that even their spittle is described as being in agreement. As mentioned in a preceding section, Mooney and Olbrechts (1932:15) report that saliva is an extremely potent aspect of traditional Cherokee medicine and, according to their interpretation, ranked equally with blood in importance. Invoking spittle as a measure of or a vehicle for the agreement for the fisherman and the fish indicates that they are approaching oneness. This symbolic manifestation of the relationship between people and the animals in their environment reflects the reciprocity between people and animals. That the fish have agreed to become prey indicates their acknowledgement of the relationship and their willingness to participate. Mooney (1900a) asserts that the phrase "white food" in the formula contextualizes the bait within the language used to refer to dishes prepared for the Green Corn ceremony, and thus assures the fish of its nutritiousness. This view also assumes that the fish share the cultural beliefs and knowledge of the fisherman and make the same associations.

Even in that time, the language used in the formula was considered archaic and very specialized. Mooney's annotations indicate that without Swimmer's instructions, translation would have been difficult. By the time Fogelson conducted his fieldwork, he found that hunting and fishing formulae were no longer in use (1961:222), and indeed today fishing formulae seem to have completely faded from use. It is reported among community members that certain individuals may still know fishing medicine, and one speaker reported having witnessed an elder chewing an unknown substance and saying something to himself before a successful fishing trip, but no one I spoke to reported knowing the details.

Fishing Signs: Perceived Ecological Relationships Between Fish and Other Natural Phenomena

Members of the North Carolina Cherokee community still contextualize freshwater fishes of the area within the body of their traditional ecological knowledge. The extensive and active Cherokee knowledge of local fish, both as a resource and as a feature of the spiritual world, is encoded in a native environmental semiology of fishing signs. In order to be able to read the environment, one must comprehend the system of relationships that it embodies, an ability that is derived from generations of observation and experimentation and is passed on culturally. Interviews with younger people who have been away from the Boundary and come back reveal that if they fish, they still know or have learned from their contemporaries the natural signs of fishing cycles.

When I was introduced to an older woman as someone who was studying Cherokee fishing, she said "Oooh, there's a lot to that. You gotta know the signs." Everyone I interviewed mentioned "the signs" of fishing. In practical terms, fishing signs are cues from the seasons of the year, the environment, lunar cycles, weather, and even the time of day that inform anglers of auspicious fishing times. Some signs are as simple as knowing that the best times to fish are in the morning and the evening, while other signs depend on recognition of the correlation between flowering seasons and spawning runs. One speaker described his grandfather's knowledge of what he called "the cardinal signs" as being similar to an unwritten calendar.

There are several fishing signs that correlate flowering plants with spawning fish. As arbitrary as the signs in any semiotic system, fishing signs draw their meaning from cultural traditions. Because fish spawn and flowers bloom in the spring, it is possible to make a number of associations between events. However, people who fish Cherokee waters assign significance to relationships between particular flowers and particular fish. For example, the woman I interviewed about fish poisoning also reported that flutterfish (probably spawning *Campostoma anomalum,* perceived as different from the same fish the rest of the year) were associated with a particular flower, probably the trout lily (*Erythroni americanum*) which blooms March through May (Niering et al. 1979:598). "And then there was, I guess about in the spring, when this flower, I don't know what it's called in English, but in Cherokee it's called *uhtolv,* when that started blooming, it blooms in the spring, then these fish would spawn but they would turn as red as your shirt." Thus, the association of the sign and its referent in the mind of the speaker is apparent. There are other similar associations between flowering plants and fish runs with some variation. In at least one other case, different speakers recognize one sign to represent the presence of the same fish. One person I interviewed reported a connection between the bloom time of mountain laurel (*Kalmia latifolia*) and the spawning time of redhorse, while another reported a connection between the blooming of blackberry bushes and redhorse spawning runs.

Other fishing signs include knowledge of baits preferred by particular fish and bait hatching times, and an ability to read shadows and shade. It is not clear whether these particular aspects of the local environmental knowledge are traditional or derived from the Euro-American fly-fishing culture, which has exerted a strong influence on the fishing culture in the area. Fly fishermen are well aware of the hatching times of various flies and insects because that knowledge allows them to choose the right bait for the right moment in time. The younger generation of Cherokee fly fishermen sometimes knows the science of fly-fishing but not the traditional ideas about fish and the environment. Fly-fishing in this area is almost exclusively associated with trout fishing, which would seem to indicate a relatively recent attention to these aspects of the environment. When using traditional fishing methods, like traps, weirs, fish poisons, or even spears, one need not worry about bait hatching and water or weather conditions.

Native Natural History: Perceptions of Fish and Their Behavior

In the various fields of biology, natural history refers to observations of the life cycle of a particular plant or animal. These observations are contextualized within Western scientific ideas and used to test hypotheses and formulate new understandings of the behavior being observed. In what I term native natural history, observations are contextualized within the cosmology of a people and are used to develop understandings of behavior as well. However, the cosmological orientation of native natural histories allows for hypotheses and understandings that include possibilities outside the realm of what is possible in Western science. In the Cherokee construction of natural history, generally, transformation is a regular process of the life cycle of many animals, including some people. In the Cherokee natural history of fish, transformation is a significant theme.

On many levels fish are liminal beings, moving from one condition to another. Most obviously, they transform their colors, shapes, and appearance between spawning seasons, and consequently individual species are difficult to perceive in one state of being. In addition, hybridization between related species can give the appearance of transformation by giving rise to new, previously unseen species or subspecies of fish (Rohde et al. 1994). On a mythological level, fish inhabit the threshold between the upper world and underworld. They use the same pathways and routes of travel as the creatures of the underworld, yet we have access to them in this world. Thus fish are shady characters. However, if we understand the contexts in which fish are held to be transformational creatures and use those as avenues for exploration of empirical natural histories, we see some fascinating parallels.

The stories presented in this section exemplify aspects of Cherokee traditional ecological knowledge as it relates to the natural history of fish and shows the liminal qualities of fish that transform themselves from fish into birds and from one species of fish into another. The first story, from Mooney, shows that the idea of transformation has a historical basis and also serves as a point of comparison to the stories I have gathered in my own fieldwork.

In the 1890s, Mooney (1900a) collected a story about the sudden appearance and disappearance of a flock of unusual birds in the Qualla area. His informants enthusiastically related the story to him as though it had recently happened, when in fact it had happened forty years before. They recounted the appearance of the birds, "pale blue, with red in places [. . .] nearly the size of a crow, and [with] a long forked tail like that of a fish," and the behavior of the birds, "[they] preyed upon hornets, which [they] took upon the wing, and also feasted on the larvae in the nests," and they remembered the name the birds had been given, "*tsundigwuntsugi* or *tsundig-wuntski,* [or] 'forked' . . . referring to the tail" (285). What is most interesting to us about this account in the context of traditional ecological knowledge is the fact that the people who saw these birds explained their sudden appearance and disappearance by saying that these birds were really transformed redhorse (*Moxostoma sp.?,* Cherokee *oliga*). The forked tail, coloring, and other physical features of the redhorse that resemble the bird are apparent in photographs.

As to diet, redhorse regularly eat crustaceans and insects. Mooney (1900a) said, "It is even maintained that about the time those birds first appeared some hunters on Oconaluftee saw seven of them sitting on the limb of a tree and they were still shaped like a red-horse, although they already had wings and feathers" (285). Not only was the transformation from fish to bird possible; people actually saw it in the process of happening. He goes on to point out that the bird was undoubtedly the scissortailed flycatcher, a species native to Texas and the surrounding areas but which has been known to stray east.

The excerpt from Mooney shows that in terms of the traditional ecological knowledge being expressed, people have an exacting knowledge of the animals expected to be present in the local environment. The bird is uncommon to the area (although it has recently been spotted in Georgia) and is immediately noticed. The direct association of the bird with the red-horse fish reveals an intimate knowledge of the local fishes and a familiarity with their anatomy and behavior. Further, this association also demonstrates an understanding of the spiritual connection between the two creatures. Transformation is an acceptable explanation because it builds on observation, it falls within the realm of possibility in the traditional cosmology, and wherein fish are metamorphic creatures by nature.

Forty years after a single season of observation, the unusual event remains a part of the oral history and takes on further significance by incorporating the hunters as ancestors or community members who were actual witnesses. The story also takes on spiritual significance with reference to the number seven—a sacred number. There are seven redhorse/flycatchers on the limb of the tree, a sign that shows that this tale, initially an explanation of an aberrant event, is in the process of being mythologized. In this story, traditional ecological knowledge is at work transmitting, maintaining, and applying meaning to this unusual event.

During the course of my fieldwork, I have been privileged to learn a lot about Cherokee beliefs about fish from elicitation and from talking about fish and fishing with people who really enjoy it. I have been especially interested in understanding the connection between stories people have told me about fish behavior and the natural history of particular species of fish. While there is not necessarily a direct relationship between the two, complicated aspects of the natural history are often provided with cosmological explanations that reflect a belief in the magical properties of fish and of nature generally. During the course of one interview, the person I was interviewing and I were looking at pictures of fish and talking about the names when he pointed to one and said, "This one has a fish bed and it gathers little pebbles and makes a little mound of pebbles. There's some minnows that come to this bed, they probably hatched out in this bed. This big red belly, he blows juice through those knots and sprays those little babies. And when he sprays them they turn red into what we call a red minnow and we never knew what kind of a fish they were but there'd be a big bed of red minnows, we called them. And I think they turned into a silverside fish. I don't know what the history is to that. All I know is that my dad used to say 'he's spraying 'em.' "

In this short passage, traditional ecological knowledge of fish, their breeding habits, and their behavior is again used to explain the appearance of magical transformation. Again there is an intimate and practical knowledge of the environment, a knowledge that results from extended observation and theorizing, and the connection of that practical knowledge to the spiritual realm in the fact that the cosmology allows for the possibility of transformation. Mooney records a similar set of beliefs in an account of fish behavior from his interviews. He did not seek to identify specifically the fish species involved. Consequently, he assumes that the parent fish in the story is the *Campostoma anomalum* or Central Stoneroller. The speaker who shared his knowledge with me identified the parent species as *Nocomis micropogon* or the River Chub, a fish that has a similar appearance during both spawning and nonspawning seasons. The speaker I worked with even commented on the similarity in their appearance but made the distinction that the river chub (as identified by photo) is the fish that he is specifically talking about.

The natural history of *Nocomis micropogon* fits more closely with the description of spawning behavior found in both Mooney's and the speaker's reports. While the stoneroller does in fact roll stones and turn red at spawning, the river chub is specifically known to make large (some extremely large) nests with pebbles. Fish of other species, including minnows, also lay their eggs in the nest. The speaker identified the rosyside dace, *Clinostomus funduloides,* a small, mostly red fish in the minnow family, as the red minnow he was referring to. Any number of other closely related species may do the same, and this could be the explanation for the speaker's comment about the red minnows turning into silversides. Nest sharing is also a conduit for the hybridization of these related fish, and that could be compounding the appearance of transformation. In the Mooney account (1900a), this same fish does not transform other fish by spraying them but rather is transformed into a salamander (or spring lizard), which is similarly colored.

The last story is not as neatly concluded as the other two. In this case, the story is not about a transformation; there is no actual acknowledgment that one thing changes into another, but rather there is an underlying idea that two different creatures are really the same. The natural history points up some interesting parallels that reflect traditional ecological knowledge at work behind the scenes. Toward the end of one interview I asked the speaker if he knew any good fish stories, and he told me the story mentioned earlier about the giant eel that lives out near Murphy, at the bottom of a pool in the river, comes up, and swallows a child who was playing on the bank. (I asked and was assured that this was not the *uktena* but just a giant eel.) Later, two boys decide that they are going to kill the eel and stoneboil it to death by rolling a huge superheated boulder down into the pool.

The story goes on in great detail about how they commit this and other acts against the giant eel. At the conclusion of the story, the speaker says, "and that's why they call Murphy *Tlanusiyi* 'place of the leeches.'" Up to this point leeches had not been mentioned in the story, yet it had not occurred to me because I was so caught up in the story. As I listened to and transcribed the story later, however, it became apparent that the last line of the story was the first mention of leeches. A similar story is attested in Mooney in which Cherokees were warned from water near Murphy because a giant leech would rise up out of the water and eat them. In Cherokee, *tlanusi* is leech and *tlvdegwa* is eel, so I could not attribute the confusion to a question of translation or lexical similarity. I began to look at the natural history of eels and leeches to see if there was some connection there.

Eels, or most likely mountain brook lampreys, have a complex spawning cycle. Part of this cycle is the immature stage of the animal or ammocoete stage during which they live in the mud at pool bottoms for up to eight years, much as leeches do. Perhaps this place-name and folktale reflect an understanding of the common habitat of these animals or maybe a belief that the immature stage of the lamprey and the leech are the same creature. In subsequent interviews with the same speaker, he clarified that the story was supposed to be about leeches and that he knew of no relationship between the two. However, another speaker pointed out, without prompting, that the leech and the eel are quite similar in appearance and wondered if they were related.

Summary

This chapter documents the traditional knowledge and cosmology of fishing in the North Carolina Cherokee community. While traditional medical beliefs have largely been supplanted by Western medicine, certain fish-related taboos are still maintained. Although it has become largely a recreational enterprise, fishing is still an important part of Cherokee life.

The people interviewed for this research, even those who had been away and returned to the reservation, have maintained an understanding of the ecological relationships among species, seasons, and fish behavior. The relationships that compose a particular ecology are still perceived to some degree as rooted in the cosmological conception of the environment. Despite changes in religious practice over the past 300 years, among the people I spoke to there remains a widely held view of the environment that is at least somewhat consistent with traditional views about the nature of the world. This view is reflected in folklore, traditional ecological knowledge, and native natural histories of fish.

While even among older speakers the Cherokee names for specific fish are increasingly difficult to recall, it was still possible to catalogue the vast majority of fish that have traditional significance either in the diet or in medical practice. The exceptions are fish that have become increasingly rare or extirpated altogether through environmental change. In addition to the catalogue of names, stories from the Mooney era were documented as still being used to explain the natural world.

5
Tourism, Fishing, and Contemporary Cherokee Identity
The Discourse of Enterprise and Reserve

Tourism is an essential component of the contemporary Cherokee economy and must be considered in any ethnographic account that seeks to describe aspects of the lives of members of the Eastern Band of Cherokee Indians today. In addition to the economic forces that tourism brings to bear on tribal members, notions of representation, identity, and authenticity are all negotiated within the context of tourism. This chapter uses the practice of fishing as a portal through which to examine all of these aspects of contemporary Cherokee life and uses cultural and linguistic examples to illustrate the ways in which fishing is both an aspect of the tourist economy and an aspect of Cherokee identity. In addition, this chapter shows, through lexical data, the separation between Cherokee fishing practices and those of their non-Indian mountain neighbors. This separation, which allows an additional distinction beyond the Cherokee and non-Cherokee tourist divergences in contemporary Cherokee identity construction, also reflects an area of culture in which the traditional practices of Cherokees and mountain whites remained distinct.

The Anthropology of Tourism and Tourism in Cherokee, North Carolina

The anthropology of tourism is a relatively recent innovation in anthropological inquiry and has experienced developments and changes of perspective in the nearly three decades since its inception as a program of study. Initially, anthropologists interested in examining the multifarious aspects of tourism found themselves caught in the conflict between those advocating tourism, those cautioning against the impacts of tourism, and those insisting that tourism must only be practiced as a community-centered, nondestructive industry. Because each of these "platforms" argues a particular position, none allows for observations of tourism with a focus on gathering knowledge of its structures, processes, and functions. Thus, academic researchers have developed the "knowledge platform" of tourism studies in order to understand in a systematic way as much as possible about tourism, the largest global industry today. Naturally, the anthropological aspect of this system of inquiry focuses on the human component and on host and guest relations (Jafari 2001).

In developing the anthropological paradigm for investigating tourism, Smith (2001) delineates four dimensions to be used as tools for constructing an ethnography of tourism: habitat, history, heritage, and handicrafts. She argues that each of these dimensions contributes depth and breadth to the collection of data and their analysis. Certainly these dimensions play crucial roles in describing Cherokee tourism and contextualizing fishing as one of its aspects.

The habitat for Cherokee tourism, as described in Chapter 2, is a highly charismatic feature. Mountains, forests, waterways and waterfalls, cliffs, rhododendron balds, and alpine meadows all draw visitors to the area. The unique qualities of the habitat of western North Carolina and east Tennessee are sought by those seeking serenity, beauty, and, important for this research, outdoor recreational activities. The waters, in particular, draw anglers from all over the eastern United States and contribute a considerable sum to the local economy (half a million dollar in permits alone).

The history component of Smith's model refers to the history of the relationships between the tourist community members and outsiders. Members of the Cherokee community have been in contact with outsiders for hundreds of years, and the history of that contact colors the tourist interchange. Colonization, missionization, the Removal, the fight for land, the Gilded Age expansion of tourism, prejudice, and economic interdependence all have roles in the complex interchange of tourism and the construction of identity. For example, the casino, a popular tourist destination and economic boon to North Carolina Cherokee and non-Cherokee communities alike, is legally possible only because of the history of the relationship between two sovereign nations, the United States and the Eastern Band of Cherokee Indians, and the relationship between the Eastern Band and the State of North Carolina.

Heritage, the third aspect of Smith's paradigm, is a central component of the majority of the tourism that transpires on the Qualla Boundary. However, while Smith is referring to the use, by community members, of items of heritage in the tourism industry, which is amply evident in Cherokee, there is an additional aspect of heritage in Cherokee tourism. Tourists, especially those from the Southeast, often come to Cherokee to discover or have contact with their own heritage. The notion that many individuals have at least one Cherokee ancestor is common in the Southeast and can be traced to different aspects of the history of the interchange between Cherokees and Euro-Americans, including early intermarriages. The complex history, often further complicated by family legends, coupled with the romanticization of Native American identity by some non-Cherokees, leads thousands of visitors each year to pore over the various Removal rolls looking for the names of relatives so that they might prove their Cherokee heritage.

In addition to the rolls from Removal times, there are also rolls that were devised as part of the 1906 land claim settlement over the sale of the so-called Love tract, tens of thousands of acres east by northeast of the present-day Qualla Boundary that were sold for timber. When the enrollment figures were calculated by Guion Miller, an attorney for the Indian Agency, for this land sale, they included nearly 30,000 people, only about 3,000 of whom lived east of the Mississippi. This calculation left the per capita payout from the sale at just over $133, and while this roll was later disputed by the tribe, many people still attribute what they know of their ancestry to it (Finger 1991). Heritage tourism is a booming business, and tracing one's genealogy is often a central part of a visit to Cherokee. Evidence for this phenomenon can be seen on the tribe's website, which has an entire page devoted to offering advice on tracing one's Cherokee roots. Still others visit Cherokee to observe and learn about Cherokee culture and heritage as it is presented in the Museum of the Cherokee Indian, the Oconaluftee Indian Village (a living history museum), and the outdoor drama "Unto These Hills." Thus, heritage is a multifaceted component of tourism in Cherokee.

Handicrafts are also a significant constituent of Cherokee tourism and the last piece of Smith's model. The Qualla Mutual is a craft cooperative that promotes traditional crafts made by local artisans. This high end of the handicraft market includes basketry, carvings, pottery, and other examples of Cherokee craft traditions, as well as jewelry, household items, and toys. Among community members there is a great deal of pride in the native crafts, and, as Hill (1997) has shown, baskets especially are still manufactured and used by local people themselves as a way of delineating authentic Cherokee identity from tourist stereotypes. The Museum of the Cherokee Indian also has a gift shop that sells baskets and other Cherokee crafts, in addition to books, T-shirts, and other souvenirs. At the opposite end of the spectrum are the trinkets sold in the shops on the tourist strips on U.S. 441 and U.S. 19. These stores and the attractions that surround them reflect an active manipulation of the stereotypes of "Indianness" that tourists expect to see. The irony of tourists visiting one of the few actual native commu-

Figure 5.1. Billboard on U.S. 441 in Jackson County, North Carolina, promoting fishing on the Qualla Boundary.

nities in the East and passing over beautiful traditional crafts in favor of cheap rubber tomahawks, Minnetonka moccasins, and feathered headdresses is not lost on community members.

Fishing as a Cherokee Tourism Business

Between sunrise and sunset every day from the last Saturday of March through the end of the following February (yes, more than eleven months out of the year), anglers line up along the waterways of the Qualla Boundary. The business of fishing is alive and well on these tribal waters, as shown by the more than half a million dollars worth of fishing permits issued on the Boundary each year. Tribal ordinance requires that the trout stocking program be financially self-sufficient through permit sales. Currently prices for fishing permits start at $7 per day up to $200 for an annual pass, and permits are available from more than twenty-eight local businesses (Figure 5.1). Beyond fishing permits, anglers desire many conveniences, and the tribe and local entrepreneurs do profitable business making those conveniences widely available (Maney 2002).

In order to administer the business of fishing, the tribe manages thirty miles of enterprise waters as a component of their tourist industry. Tribal resource managers breed and stock tribal enterprise waters with between 300,000 and 400,000 fish each year, including a certain number of enormous record-challenging trout and novelty albino rainbow trout. In 1984, the EBCI constructed its own surface water fish hatchery to meet the growing demand for fish. Rainbow, brown, and mountain brook trout are all stocked in tribal enterprise waters, and all stocked fish are raised from the several hundred thousand fish eggs the tribe obtains annually from the National Fish Hatchery in Erwin, Tennessee (Maney 2002).

Surface water hatcheries, such as the one constructed by the EBCI, use natural well water that is exposed to the elements in raceways, or long, narrow, outdoor holding tanks. Each different species is separated into stages of development in the raceways, with particular areas reserved for the specialty fish mentioned. Once the fish reach a certain size, they are moved up to the next pen until they ultimately progress to stocking size. Surface water hatcheries of this kind are difficult to maintain because there is no control over the temperature or other water qualities while the water is in the open raceways. For example, in the winter a Game and Fish agent must spend the night at the hatchery whenever a freeze is possible in order to keep the water flowing in the raceways. The tribal hatchery is also subject to EPA regulations on water quality at the discharge point where water leaves the raceways and enters Raven's Fork, where it must be free of any solid waste produced by the fish. Despite these challenges, the tribe manages the hatchery successfully, providing all of the fish stocked in the Boundary waters each year (Maney 2002).

Tourism, Space, and the Negotiation of Identity

Eastern Cherokee community members construct their identity within the context of the tourist economy, which, as outlined above, presents a variety of elements that must be incorporated, ignored, or rejected. The use of space on the reservation is a significant assertion of the boundaries between locals and tourists, between Cherokees and non-Cherokees. This section will consider the use of space as an element in drawing those boundaries within the tourist milieu, along with some of the features of tourism in Cherokee that make the negotiation of space critical.

To understand spatial arrangements on the Qualla Boundary, some description of the space is in order. Highways U.S. 441 and U.S. 19 are the two major thoroughfares on which visitors reach Cherokee, and the intersection of these two routes is the virtual epicenter for the explosion of tourism in the town of Cherokee (Figure 5.2). From this point one can look in any direction and see an array of images: cartoon Indian theme shops, tribal

Figure 5.2. Tourist traffic on U.S. 441 in downtown Cherokee. This photo was taken on Memorial Day weekend, the first weekend of the summer tourist season.

offices, a tribal park, the elementary school, churches, gas stations, and restaurants, all set in an exquisitely beautiful valley with a broad river at its center. Along U.S. 19 lie the tribal bingo hall, Santa's Land (an amusement park and zoo), the casino/hotel/conference center area, RV parks, a grocery store, a scenic chairlift, and ultimately, if one keeps driving, the Kituwah archaeological site. The elementary school, the tribal offices, the council house, the ceremonial grounds, the museum, the craft cooperative, the Cherokee Historical Society, and eventually the Great Smoky Mountains National Park are all arrayed along U.S. 441. Starting near the intersection of U.S. 441 with U.S. 19, Acquoni Road runs roughly parallel to, and across the Oconaluftee River from, U.S. 441. Acquoni Road is the home of the high school, tribal justice offices, the Head Start program, the satellite campus of Western Carolina University, and the tribal housing authority. Up the river from downtown Cherokee, U.S. 441 and Acquoni Road intersect, and Big Cove Road emerges from that intersection running northeast while U.S. 441 continues northwest on through the Great Smoky Mountains National Park. Although there are tourist-oriented businesses scattered among all of the businesses and offices, they are primarily concentrated in the mile of U.S. 19 east of its intersection with U.S. 441 and the mile of U.S. 441

north of that same intersection. In that area one can find a number of businesses that trade in a variety of images of Indianness.

The images and representations of Indianness prepared for tourist consumption run the gamut from beautiful baskets, carvings, pottery, and other crafts handmade by enrolled members of the tribe, to tomahawks, drums, and other toys mass-produced by the tribe for sale in the western North Carolina tourist areas, to tourist trinkets manufactured in Asia. As Bender (1996) points out, even the syllabary, which is venerated and appreciated by community members for its unique importance in the culture, has been commodified into coffee mugs, T-shirts, and keychains. This section describes some of the representations of Indianness in Cherokee and shows their relationship to Cherokee culture and language.

One of the most remarkable representations of Indianness in the town of Cherokee is the practice of chiefing. In chiefing, individuals wear multicolored, vaguely Plains-style war bonnets, sit in canvas or metal tepees to have photos made with tourists, and thus sell a reified stereotypical image of Indianness to tourists. This practice is remarkable because people come from literally all over the world to take pictures with the chiefs (French 1998), evidence that tourists are interested in buying what they expect to see, even if those images or items are completely unrelated to the local culture (tepees and war bonnets were never a part of Cherokee culture until chiefing). Chiefing has now become a tradition of the tourist culture, and tourists expect the chiefs to be there from year to year, with some families even having generations of pictures with chiefs. Chiefing has also become a part of the local culture and economy, with successful chiefs supporting their own families during the tourist season with the income they earn at a few dollars a picture. The stereotypical images of Indianness endure from the early days of the tourist trade when they were initially used to draw visitors to the area and have become a type of cultural tradition themselves.

Chiefing occurs only in the tourist shop areas of the reservation on U.S. 19 and U.S. 441. On these strips, the stereotypical and cartoonish images of Indianness are commonplace, and the representations made by the chiefs appear to fit in. In this area, the businesses press themselves against the road and each other, often sharing common walls, and sometimes only a line of parking spaces separates their front doors from the highway. The shops in the tourist areas are covered with insistent signage (some with neon, most with large capital letters) announcing their names, their contents and the deals they have to offer. The visual experience is overwhelming.

The spaces reserved for the conduct of tribal business, however, are removed from the tourist areas, even if just by being oriented with their doors turned away from the road. The tribal council house, for example, while technically on U.S. 441, is set back from the road with its entrance facing the ceremonial ground. Unless a person has business with the tribal council, he or she might pass it by altogether. The Cherokee Fairground, which serves as a mixed tourist and local space, faces the road but has recently been renovated to include a stonework wall and entry facade to separate it from the always busy road. Even before the new facade was put in place, a fence and a partial wall blocked the view into the fairground from the road.

The offices of the police department and the game and fish department, and other offices for tribal business are on a hill above the tribal council office, still in town but even further removed from the tourist areas. The private spaces of the reservation, especially residences, are most often far removed from the tourist spaces, which allows the conduct of everyday life in a space not surrounded by tourists and the images and representations of Indianness manufactured for their consumption. First-time visitors to the area are often altogether unaware of the tribal offices and private areas of the reservation.

Beyond the negotiation of physical space to separate tourist, official, and private areas of the reservation, stereotypical images of Indianness are countered in the representations of contemporary Cherokee programs and issues in the signage on the reservation, most notably billboards. Naturally, there are billboards advertising restaurants, shops, and other attractions, but there are also billboards addressed specifically to Cherokee people about diabetes prevention, domestic violence intervention programs, and the importance of preserving the cultural heritage of the Cherokee community. The billboards, while a form of public discourse, also establish a contemporary cultural boundary. Through this signage, Cherokee people are represented as being concerned with many of the same issues as their neighbors and the tourists themselves. This representation mitigates both the perception of Cherokee people as trapped in the late-19th-century ethnographic present and romanticized perceptions of contemporary Native American life. However, at the same time, the signage draws a cultural boundary because the Cherokee community is addressed specifically and outsiders are not included.

Outsiders are invited to experience representations of Cherokee traditional culture, at least to a measured extent. The Museum of the Cherokee Indian offers everything from holographic images of Cherokee cosmology, to museum exhibits of Cherokee history and culture, to a bookstore and gallery. Visitors are educated through the museum about Cherokee life from archaeological times up to the early 20th century. Across the street from the museum, the Qualla Mutual craft cooperative has its own displays of traditional craft and textile history, as well as contemporary crafts for sale to serious collectors and those casually interested in indigenous art and upscale souvenirs. Up the mountain from the museum are the Oconaluftee Indian Village, a living history village that re-creates Cherokee life from the late 18th century to the early 19th, and the massive amphitheater that is the home of *Unto These Hills,* an outdoor drama that vividly recounts the events leading up to and following the Trail of Tears. In each of these attractions, aspects of Cherokee heritage are made accessible to the thousands of tourists who pour through the area every day in summer.

Text and Talk about Fishing as a Context for Negotiating Boundaries

While the public aspects of Cherokee heritage and history that are on display draw large numbers of visitors to the area, the Qualla Boundary and its communities, as mentioned earlier, are home to nearly 13,000 people. As described, the enrolled members, as a distinct ethnic group surrounded by and interacting regularly with outsiders, negotiate boundaries between themselves and others through a number of strategic methods. Public and private discourse about fishing, the environment, and the management of the local waters are one such method. The rest of this chapter will examine the ways in which talk and texts about fish and fishing act as ethnic boundary markers, forming one small part of Cherokee identity.

Public and private discourse about fishing are two ways in which Cherokee anglers separate their own identity from that of the commercialized images of Indianness that permeate portions of the Qualla Boundary, as described in the preceding section. Texts about fishing, or at least "text-artifacts" as defined by Silverstein and Urban (1996), which are available to tourists and non-Cherokees who live near the Boundary, include the public discourse of the brochure which outlines the regulations for fishing on the reservation, interviews with Cherokee anglers and Department of Game and Fish employees in the newspaper, and even coverage by cable television's ESPN2 of a recent children's fishing derby. Discourse in each of these contexts associates fishing with traditional Cherokee values and practices but at the same time provides a view of contemporary Cherokee life. Private interviews with individual community members also delineate the relationship between authenticity and fishing. This section comprises an analysis of discourse from each of these contexts and shows a negotiation between the desire to attract tourists to the area, the necessity of maintaining a separate Cherokee identity, and the role that fishing plays in each.

The fishing regulation brochure provides a public context for delineation between the cultural heritage of the Cherokee people, the pastime of fishing, and efforts to attract tourists with both. Embodying all four features of tourism set forth by Smith (2001), the brochure is also a text, or text-artifact, by which we can understand the social and cultural processes at work when it was inscribed (Silverstein and Urban 1996). As such, declarations of hospitality and ethnic pride are in a dynamic tension that is evident in the brochure itself. It prominently features photographs of the natural beauty of the area, anglers fishing, a map of the tribal enterprise waters, and three important representations of Cherokee traditional values and identity as they relate to fishing. On the front cover is a photograph of a beautiful young woman holding a river cane basket and wearing a calico dress with ribbon trim, a beaded hair ornament similar to the crowns awarded in local pageants, and a corn bead necklace. Each of these articles (with the exception of the crown) represents traditional 19th-century Cherokee women's dress, and these are items still worn in local pageants and talent contests.

The presence of the young woman on the brochure in these clothes signifies that trout fishing in Cherokee is to be perceived as a wholesome activity, one that is strongly identified with traditional aspects of Cherokee culture. The photograph markets the habitat, history, heritage, and handicrafts of Cherokee to prospective anglers. Above the photograph the brochure reads "Enjoy Trout Fishing in the Mountains of the Cherokee" and beneath it "We welcome you to the homelands of the Cherokee and hope you enjoy fishing or just the peace and beauty of our rivers." Each phrase iterates the notion of an invitation into a private space, which, when read together with the photograph, bids visitors to take part in an aspect of Cherokee cultural heritage.

The second image of traditional identity is a picture of a mountain brook trout. It is the only trout native to the area, and while brook trout are stocked by the tribe, they are harder to raise and less easily caught than the rainbow and brown trout (Maney 2002). The native range of brook trout is in water that is higher and colder than the range of the rainbow and brown trout. Thus, the use of the brook trout in the brochure signifies an identification of the trout and its range with Cherokee cultural heritage, but it also refers the viewer to less commonly traveled areas of the Boundary.

The third representation of traditional culture in the brochure is a photo of an oak split fish basket next to a fly rod. The image is significant because traditional Cherokee fish baskets are not likely to be used or even recognized by most anglers, but they are an important aspect of authentic Cherokee identity. This single image reflects the adaptation of traditional practices and crafts to changes in the environment, technology, and subsistence. While the fish basket is a traditional form, its construction from oak is a relatively recent innovation, one that occurred in conjunction with the diminishing of river cane supplies. The shape of the fish basket has also changed, becoming wider at the opening and larger overall. This may relate to the change in materials, but it may also reflect a change in the use to which fish baskets are often put today. Rather than being specifically for the transportation of fish, which would require a tight opening to keep the fish from leaping out, these baskets are often used today for general purposes, such as purses. The narrow opening of the traditional fish basket would make it inconvenient to use as a purse. Finally, the fish that most people catch today are the stocked rainbow and brown trout, which are considerably larger than the brook trout of traditional times. These innovations together with the juxtaposition of the fish basket and the fly rod can be seen as a metaphor for contemporary Cherokee identity. Traditional ideas and practices are held onto but are adapted to incorporate new technologies.

The call to experience the practice of traditional fishing is fortified further in the brochure with these words:

> We invite you to fish here in our ancestral home lands. . . .
>
> In these streams our fore fathers and mothers have fished for untold years. . . .
>
> Even before these lands around you now were known as 'The Great Smoky Mountains,' when they were known to us as 'The Land of the Blue Mist' . . .
>
> But come, join us, the Native Americans, in the art of trout fishing.

These lines encompass several contrasting aspects of identity and tourism. There is in the first phrase a reiteration of the invitation seen on the cover, an invitation that at once draws visitors and accents the fact that the invitation is to someone's home. In the next line, the brochure emphasizes the longevity of the traditional culture, pointedly including both male and female ancestors. The word "foremothers" seems at first to be a reflection of a modern feminist reinterpretation of history, but it is indicative of the complementarity between men and women in traditional and contemporary Cherokee culture. In this line and the next two, the brochure conveys the sense that Cherokee culture is as old as the mountains themselves, older than the name Great Smoky Mountains. The final phrase begins with the adversarial conjunction "but," which reflects the contrary juxtaposition of the longevity of the culture with the following additional invitation, the crux of the tension between tourism and cultural heritage. The use of "but" here implies a sense that Cherokee cultural heritage will prevail despite tourism and a sense of the tolerance and generosity in the Cherokee community. The final phrase also contains a self-reference as Native Americans, a name very rarely used in everyday self-identification. The use of the term Native Americans erects a formal and somewhat distant cultural boundary between Cherokee and tourist and clearly separates the in-group of those with Cherokee ancestry from the others.

The brochure also reveals that the negotiation of space with respect to tourists pertains to fishing as well. While the tribe manages thirty miles of enterprise waters for use by tourists, the remaining waters are reserved for enrolled members of the tribe. These areas include many of the headwaters of streams and creeks and most of the waters near residential areas. In addition, while the brochure specifies the methods to be used by tourists and others who buy fishing permits and fish in the enterprise waters, traditional practices are still allowed in the waters reserved for tribe members. Certainly fewer people use the reserved waters and practices because of the prevalence of stocked fish in the enterprise waters, but interviews indicate that the availability of the reserved waters and practices is a point of pride and self-identity.

The private discourse of interviews with community members indicates that these waters are conceived of as an authentic part of Cherokee life that is separate from tourist fishing. As I discussed the survival of a certain species of fish with one person, the separation of enterprise waters, reserved waters, and national park waters became apparent, as well as an identification among the reserved waters, native fish, and traditional ways. In this interview, a woman from Big Cove explained about the beloved fish of her childhood, the flutterfish. "But you don't see those flutterfish anymore not the red ones. . . . Because of the stock trout they put in the waters, they eat up all the small, you very seldom find minnows, except where I live. Now I live way up above the enterprise waters."

The exception of herself and her family home from the stocked waters is an important assertion of authentic identity. Native fish and authentic native identity are necessarily removed from the tourist areas and kept separate. The flutterfish and minnows were, at times, crucial to survival when the economy was lean, but now they are uncommon because of the fish stocked for tourism, a metaphor for the replacement of one means of survival by another.

As this same interview continued, additional differences were delineated between tourist spaces and native spaces, tourist fish and native fish. I asked her about the fish stocking and which areas were reserved for enrolled members. "You can still find flutterfish up where I live and on a little bit above there, of course, in ten minutes above where my family lives, you're in the national park. You're not allowed to fish there anyway; of course, you know, park rangers don't go up our way."

This passage makes apparent the connection between the land and water of the national park and the idea of land unspoiled by tourists and the stocked fish necessary to draw them to the area. Fishing in the park is a controversial subject, because it is strictly regulated, much more so than fishing on the Qualla Boundary. Only since 2002 has the National Park Service opened certain streams to catching mountain brook trout. The NPS had prohibited fishing for brook trout in an effort to increase their numbers but recently decided that their efforts had made no apparent difference in the number of fish present in the creeks within the Great Smoky Mountains National Park.

The next passage shows that while the woman I interviewed clearly knows the National Park boundary, she is much less concerned with the lower reaches of the Oconaluftee River on the Qualla Boundary, because all the waters beneath the fish hatchery are populated by stocked trout. The hatchery is just above the Straight Fork Bridge. I asked, "Where does that start, where is the boundary of the enterprise waters?" "Straight Fork Bridge going towards Big Cove and I'm really not sure where it is in the other areas. Cause I know all down through Birdtown it is. But you can taste the difference in stocked trout and the native trout."

Thus the significance of the difference between native and stocked trout becomes apparent. It is not simply a matter of the space between tourists and locals but a matter of taste. When I asked her the difference between native and stocked trout, she said, "I don't even . . . the only way I'll eat stocked trout is they have to stay in the freezer. A week to four weeks. If they stay in the freezer. And then you have to scrape the scales, scrape 'em all off of the stocked trout. . . . You don't have to do that with native trout. They have a real strong fishy taste, the stocked trout do."

She is not alone in her distaste for the stocked fish. One man in his late thirties made a point of saying that he fished above the enterprise waters because the stocked fish taste "like dog food." Thus, the separation of enterprise waters and practices from traditional waters and practices, native trout and stocked trout, all reflect separations of Cherokee identity from others who fish on the Boundary. The fish highly sought after by tourists and others who visit the reservation do not taste the same as the native fish. Metaphors of tourism leaving a bad taste in the mouth of community members present themselves to mind.

On August 3, 2002, the tribe hosted the Talking Trees Children's Trout Derby, and I was one of more than 120 volunteers from the community and surrounding area. The derby happened in the waters surrounding the Oconaluftee Islands Park, or the "talking trees" park. (On the islands audio boxes at the base of a variety of native trees tell the names and natural

Figure 5.3. Participants in the 2003 Talking Trees Children's Trout Derby. Hundreds of children and their parents came from all over the Southeast to participate in the first annual event.

history of the trees in Cherokee and English, hence the name "talking trees.") The derby brought together approximately 800 children, some who were community members and others from all over the Southeast, for the sole purpose of trying to catch trout (Figure 5.3). Cable television sports channel ESPN2 covered the event in their Cumberland Stories series (of which the EBCI is a sponsor), and the host of the show interviewed a variety of people present at the event, including Chief Leon Jones, David Ensley, the Game and Fish program manager, and professional Cherokee angler Marty Fourkiller (Thompson 2002). The public discourse of these interviews reveals a community desire to bring together Cherokees and non-Cherokees and, in doing so, fight stereotypes of Indians while, at the same time, developing healthy outdoor habits with children. The dynamic tension between tourism and authentic identity is expressed in a number of aspects of the event and the discourse around it.

In the ESPN2 interview, Chief Jones affirmed that one of the primary motivations for the event, after catching fish, "is the stereotype of Indian. Maybe we can show the children that what they see on TV and what they see in movies . . . the real, the real life story of Indians." In this statement, he showed a desire to frame the event in a positive light while acknowledging the paradox inherent in drawing tourists who hold stereotypical notions of Indianness. He avoided saying anything negative about either the stereotypes or the people who believe in them by simply omitting the verb of the phrase with a pause. Thus he works around his difficult position, that of being at once interviewed on television hoping to draw more visitors to the area and trying gently to educate people about the stereotypical notions of Indian life that they might subscribe to and that exist all around town in the tourist shops. Later in the piece, he declared that children are the future and that "to do something like this for them, and the mixture we have here of Indians and non-Indians, and people from all over the south mostly, it's just a way of introducing ourselves and teaching these children something about the outdoors and something they need to know."

In this statement, Chief Jones focused only on the positive; he affirmed the mixture of peoples present for the event and presented the event as an educational opportunity, not just about the outdoors but also about "something [children] need to know." While the "something" is not specified, when taken with his earlier comments about fighting stereotypical images of Indianness, it takes on cultural significance. His statements reflect a desire to use tourism not only to make money for the community but to educate the tourists, thus promoting a construction of Indian identity as separate from essentialist or stereotypical ideas. It is important to note, however, that Chief Jones carefully avoided discussing Cherokee identity in this public, tourist-oriented discourse. While he wanted to educate tourists away from their preconceived notions about what it means to be Indian, what it meant to be Cherokee was not overtly stated. The interviews with Chief Jones were a part of the ESPN2 interview but not a part of the fishing derby, and thus the audience was perceived as being different.

The same event, however, generated a large corpus of discourse directed at the immediate local audience and included talk about fishing, Indian identity, and Cherokee identity. One piece of discourse that was included in the ESPN2 piece was footage of Marty Fourkiller, a professional fisherman and an Oklahoma Cherokee who now lives in North Carolina. He served as a crucial link between the professional fishing world (especially coverage on ESPN2) and the Cherokees. As a professional angler, Fourkiller is sponsored by various commercial entities to fish in tournaments around the country. At the fishing derby he held local celebrity status and was presented as a fishing expert to the children. In the following passage from his "secrets of fishing" talk to the children, he conveys his knowledge of fish behavior to the children. "Well, kids, I don't know that I have the secret to catching fish, it's all about learning about them, what they like. It's just kinda like us.

Why are we sitting over here doing these stories instead of sitting out there in the sun? We like the shade don't we? Well, the fish they're the same way, just like this morning when you first got in the water. I mean there were just fish coming in, but the sun was down below that hillside there, and the stream over here was shaded."

While Fourkiller did not grow up with North Carolina traditional ecological knowledge, he describes the behavior of the fish in terms that are similar to those used by consultants for this research. The fish are personified as having likes and dislikes similar to those of humans. As mentioned in the preceding chapter, in traditional Cherokee ecological knowledge, this idea can be directly related to the perception of all living things as having the same types of personalities and behaviors in their repertoires. However, in traditional ecological knowledge, fish are also portrayed as having special abilities. The fish in Fourkiller's discussion are not magical. Rather, if anything they are just small, scaly people.

As Fourkiller explains how to understand fish, he begins by saying that it is a matter of understanding what they like and dislike, then goes on to ask a question that sets up the absolute similarity between people and fish. In order to catch a fish, one must think like a fish and fish are really just like us. The personification of fish by fishermen is not a uniquely Cherokee trait, however. In my own unpublished research on discourse about fishing among fishermen on the Gulf Coast of Florida, fish are often portrayed by professional and nonprofessional anglers as worthy adversaries (Altman 1997). This construction of fish as worthy and wily adversaries drives the economy of the U.S. sportfishing industry and in some cases reaches truly mythic proportions. So while Fourkiller is certainly Cherokee and a professional fisherman, the information that he provides about fishing appears to be drawn more from his experience as a professional fisherman than as a traditional Cherokee. In contrast, local Cherokee fisherman Jerry Wolfe, one of the primary consultants for this research, was on hand at the Trout Derby to provide the Cherokee perspective on fishing; he told stories from his youth about fishing with some of the more traditional methods and gave his own versions of folktales related to fishing. In addition to the fishing instruction and fish stories, a dance group performed to Cherokee singing and drumming, thus allowing tourists a glimpse of traditional Cherokee culture not otherwise widely available.

As a whole, the fishing derby was a context in which fishing contributed to the active construction of contemporary Cherokee identity in the milieu of tourism. While Chief Jones delineated the desires and concerns of the tribe in the ESPN2 interview, the events of the day provided opportunities for individuals to show tourists the traditions of the Cherokee (through the dancing and storytelling); to show Cherokee people as active participants in the larger contemporary U.S. society (through the television coverage and material goods awarded as prizes); and to educate the public about fishing in the Cherokee homeland.

English Fish Names, a Divide between Cherokee and Non-Cherokee Locals

Every linguistic and cultural community has many voices and many ways of telling its stories. Each voice has an important role in maintaining cultural knowledge and preserving the continuity of local traditions. The Eastern Band of Cherokee Indians continues to use its many voices to maintain its rich cultural heritage, both in the native language and local varieties of English.

While knowledge of the names of local fishes in the Cherokee language is an important piece of the Traditional Ecological Knowledge on the Qualla Boundary, knowledge of the various English vernacular names for fish marks an ethnic boundary. While in the last century tourists have virtually inundated the Cherokee area for at least four months out of the year, the Eastern Cherokee have lived in close contact with European-descended peoples for more than three centuries. Naturally, there are a number of cultural features shared by the two groups, including many traditional local food preferences: gathering and eating ramps (a local variety of wild leek with an extremely potent odor and flavor); the preference for cornbread over other breads at meals; and the gathering and eating of wild greens (e.g., creasy greens, a wild green similar to watercress). However, when it comes to the consumption of fish, Cherokees and their white neighbors appear to have retained separate ideas about which fish were edible. This is apparent in interviews about fishing methods and preferences but also in the fact of the differences between groups in English vernacular names for fish.

When I interviewed non-Cherokee anglers with longstanding family traditions in the western North Carolina area, I found that while they might recognize fish other than gamefish (i.e., trout, bass, pike), they were less apt to be able to name them. When asked to identify many of the smaller fish that have English vernacular names in Cherokee, non-Cherokees generally class them all as minnows. Experienced fishermen, including one fly-fishing shop owner, call many of the nongame fishes "bait" or trash fish. One man I interviewed reported that his family had never to his knowledge traditionally eaten knottyheads, redhorse, other sucker fish, or any fish other than trout.

Local non-Cherokees recognize only the three varieties of trout as edible. In addition to these, the Cherokee people I interviewed also recognize several species of redhorse, the one local species of hogsucker, and other sucker fish as being edible, and some would say preferable. Redhorse, hogsucker, and trout were the three fish names most readily recalled in the Cherokee language among speakers. Appendix 6 shows the local Cherokee English names for eleven fish that are considered edible or otherwise significant in the folklore.

While local non-Cherokees interviewed for this project have little to no interest in nongame fish, the Cherokee speakers and English-speaking Cherokees I interviewed still maintain the English vernacular names for a wide variety of fish, a fact that reflects the continuing value of the fish as a food source. The use of the Cherokee English vernacular names for fish is an ethnic boundary that reflects traditional notions of edibility and a depth of understanding of the local ecology. In addition to their subsistence value, preference for and knowledge of these fish signals a history particular to the Cherokee people, a history that comprises a deep and abiding knowledge of their environs, a spirituality that is connected to that knowledge, a set of tastes developed in conjunction with their beliefs and history, and an active desire to delineate Cherokee culture from that of their neighbors. Food preference is often a "matter of acquired taste." When taste is acquired along with culture, language, and worldview, it becomes more than a cliché; it becomes a reflection of deeply held values and as such functions as a clear boundary between Cherokee and non-Cherokee.

Summary

In this chapter I have shown that fishing is still an aspect of defining authentic Cherokee identity in the context of the tourist environment. In addition to the economic forces that tourism brings to bear on tribal members, notions of representation, identity, and authenticity are all negotiated within the context of tourism. The anthropology of tourism provides a practical paradigm for constructing an ethnography of tourism. This chapter examines the use of space on the reservation as a part of the anthropology of tourism in Cherokee and finds that it is a significant assertion of the boundaries between Cherokees and non-Cherokees.

The negotiation of space and authenticity are both reflected in public and private discourse about fishing, the environment, and the management of the local waters. By drawing together the anthropology of tourism and how that relates to the negotiation of space on the reservation, it is possible to see how text and talk about waters reserved for use by tribal members demarcates Cherokee identity from tourists and from local non-Cherokees. Finally, in the North Carolina Cherokee community, the use of Cherokee English vernacular names for fish is a significant reflection of the separation between Cherokee and mountain non-Cherokee fishing preferences and practices.

6

Conclusions

The examination of fishing as an isolated domain allows a small but significant aperture through which to focus on Cherokee culture and language from a variety of perspectives. The insights gleaned from such a study are diverse and timely. Cherokee fishing has been virtually neglected in discussions of subsistence, language, environmental science, and recreation. Thus, in order to grasp the broad significance of fishing in Cherokee culture, this study takes up a number of issues. At its most concrete level, it comprises the first systematic documentation of Cherokee fishing from the early contact period to the present and presents information drawn from historical documents, unpublished sources, ethnographic interviews, and environmental data. The information collected in the appendixes provides expedient reference to most of the relevant data pertaining to fishing, previously hidden in obscure sources or altogether undocumented.

In addition to the documentary component of this work, it also provides a window into the basic processes of human perception and cognition of the natural environment. Fishing has served here as a particularly narrow but productive avenue for investigating the ways in which cognition, shaped by Cherokee culture and language, intertwines perceptions of the environment with subsistence practices, material culture traditions, cosmological and medical beliefs, and personal identity. The study shows that the perception and cognition of the natural world is a basis for each of these aspects of Cherokee culture.

Essential to this project is the diachronic examination of changes in the fishing environment through ethnohistorical methodology, which allows a perspective unavailable in strictly synchronic studies. Ethnohistory permits a reevaluation of historical sources, providing a more accurate picture of the past interaction between people and their environment, which, when informed by ethnography, demonstrates the relationship of that history to cultural patterns today. An understanding of the history of environmental change and its relationship to the economy and culture creates a clearer picture of subsistence practices and their adaptation. Through the lens of ethnohistory, it is possible to view change as a continuous adaptive process, rather than as a slideshow of ethnographic snapshots isolated in time and location. Environmental change functions as an index by which we can view the processes of colonization, modernization, globalization, and economic development in the Eastern Cherokee community. In this study, for example, changes in the names for fish reflect extirpations of old species and the introduction of new ones and enable me to track dramatic changes in the environment, economy, and culture. By correlating the historical linguistic data with the historical environmental data, it is possible to follow changes in Cherokee subsistence and ritual practices over time and distance. The historical linguistic data may also be of use to environmental scientists such as wildlife biologists, ecologists, and hydrologists, who will find application for this work in understanding the history of human impact on the environment and may be able to use the data to date specific events in the ecology.

While it seems intuitively obvious that fishing was at one time a significant seasonal supplement to Cherokee subsistence, that fact had never been specifically documented before now. Archaeological, historical, linguistic, and ethnographic sources provide a reflection of the importance of fishing in the traditional economy and the enormous contribution that the game fishing program makes to the tourist economy today. For example, the trout-stocking program is required by tribal ordinance to be self-supporting through permit sales and successfully generates over half a million dollars a year in permits alone. This figure does not include the retail and lodging contributions made by fishermen, which are hard to estimate. The degree of lexical and craft specialization related to fishing that is still visible in Cherokee culture today indicates the importance of fishing to the Cherokee subsistence economy. Cherokee speakers today still recognize and name a substantial number of species of fish and other edible or ritually important aquatic species as shown here. English-speaking Cherokees also recognize a significant number of species of fish and identify them with English vernacular names that are, in some cases, translations of the Cherokee names. Future linguistic research should include comparisons with both northern Iroquoian and southeastern Muskogean data on fish names and fishing practices. The comparison may well provide new perspectives on precontact movement and settlement of the Cherokee people.

This research also sheds light on why Cherokee fishing has been so difficult to see in the archaeological context, a fact that relates, in large part, to the invisibility of women's work in the archaeological and historical record.

Many of the past contributions that women have made to subsistence are not easily detectable, and those related to Cherokee fishing are no exception. Women were significant providers in the traditional Cherokee economy in ways beyond those that have been understood, as shown here. Although Cherokee women have long been recognized as excellent gatherers and agriculturalists, I have shown that traditional constructions of the act of fishing in the literature are necessarily biased by the reporter's position. For non-Cherokee men, such as Adair, Timberlake, and Mooney, fishing was understood according to European-derived models as a part of the complex of hunting behavior and thus was naturally included in their reports with hunting and other behaviors engaged in by men. My research shows, however, that, for Cherokee women, certain methods of fishing were conceived of as gathering and supplied an important source of protein to the family diet. The preparation and consumption of fish in traditional ways left little evidence behind, further obscuring the work that women did. This aspect of the research may find application in archives and museum exhibit design, so that the general public may begin to understand better the importance of the work of native women in providing for their families. Future research on gender should include an examination of other archival sources and ethnographic interviews to continue to develop our understanding of women's work.

This study provides a view of the transition from a mixed subsistence economy to a cash economy and a shift in the role that fish played from one economy to the other. Whereas fish once played a seasonally significant role in the subsistence economy, today they play a very profitable, nearly year-round role, in the cash-based tourist economy. As this economic change has transpired, especially in the past fifty years, dramatic changes in health among Cherokee people have occurred, including significant rises in the occurrence of diabetes, heart problems, and cancer (Lefler, pers. comm.). As convenience foods have become more widely available, people eat fewer and fewer traditional foods and engage in much less strenuous activity to procure them, both of which are contributing factors to the health issues faced by the tribe. Cherokee Choices, a tribal agency that administers a longitudinal study, funded by the Centers for Disease Control, on attitudes and behaviors related to health and fitness among grade school children, seeks to understand the relationship between cultural changes and the rise in health concerns. As their research develops, data regarding changing diets will be collected and could inform future research about the significance of fish in the traditional versus the contemporary diet.

Traditional medical beliefs, as well as traditional religious beliefs, and knowledge of the fishing environment have also seen dramatic change.

However, despite cultural and linguistic changes, there still exist viable avenues for the transmission of traditional cultural information. Cherokee Traditional Ecological Knowledge of fishing finds expression in Cherokee mythology, folklore, and indigenous constructions of natural history, all of which are based in the traditional cosmology and provide a rich context for understanding the values and beliefs associated with fish. This study demonstrates the depth of Cherokee fish knowledge and the interconnectedness of that knowledge with religious and medical belief. The depth of knowledge is exemplified by the fact that Cherokee speakers recognize and have a name for at least one fish, the sickle fin redhorse, which wildlife biologists have only recently begun to describe.[1] While all of the local redhorse species are desirable for food, Cherokee anglers recognize this species as separate from the other local species of redhorse because of its distinctive feathery red fin. The knowledge possessed by Cherokee fishing specialists could prove crucial to maintaining the fragile ecosystems of the area, and the tribe could benefit from applying traditional knowledge to ecosystems management. In addition, Cherokee educators may also find application for this work in constructing a native science curriculum in the local schools. The Traditional Ecological Knowledge collected here and the data in the appendixes can be used as points of comparison or as pieces in the cultural and linguistic preservation projects under way on the Qualla Boundary.

Despite the traditional relationship among fish, subsistence, cosmology, and environmental knowledge, the practice of fishing today has been reconfigured into an aspect of both the tourist economy and a pleasurable pastime for local people. The multifaceted nature of fishing provides a valuable perspective on the construction of contemporary identity in the context of tourism. Negotiation of space on the Qualla Boundary results in an ethnic boundary that separates authentic Cherokee life from the images of Indianness mass produced for public consumption. The negotiation of space is apparent in discourse about fishing, especially regarding where one may fish if one is Cherokee as opposed to where one may fish if one is not Cherokee. The reserved waters are a point of pride for local people, and they are perceived as something real, natural, and important, exclusively for tribal members. Only in those waters do the native trout thrive, and only the native trout taste right. The correlation of native trout, native waters, and authenticity provides insights into the significance of the practice of fishing in the construction of contemporary Cherokee identity. Providing an understanding of the desire of contemporary people to maintain this separation as an aspect of defining themselves is perhaps one of the most vital applications of this research.

Integrating a wide variety of sources in one research project can offer investigators insight into the various aspects of life in traditional and contemporary Native American communities. Using all of the tools of anthropology, as well as some from other disciplines, provides clearer perspectives on the agency of native peoples themselves and allows a dialogue between those perspectives and the perspectives of other people and other disciplines. As I have worked through this project I find that I have used all of my anthropological and ethnohistorical training and that the breadth of sources used here provides a depth of detail not possible through linguistic or cultural anthropology alone.

The practice of fishing is a single thread that ties together an enormous number of different aspects of Cherokee life and culture. On the most concrete level, I have found that fishing serves a variety of functions in their culture. First, it allows people purposeful time to relax and communicate with friends and family members. Next, it provides the community with free healthful food. Third, it generates nearly half a million dollars in revenue each year. Fishing also plays a role in the cosmology that is spiritually significant. Finally, fishing distinguishes a quality of authenticity among some community members and is a practice engaged in and enjoyed by almost everyone at some point in his or her life. This study demonsrates all of these aspects of Cherokee fishing. Most important, however, at a time when the Cherokee language is being replaced by English, and familiarity with traditional lifeways is diminishing, this study provides a broad yet detailed picture of an essential aspect of Cherokee traditional culture and its relationship to the changes of the past four hundred years.

Appendix 1. UNIVERSITY OF CALIFORNIA, DAVIS, Experimental Subject's Bill of Rights (Behavioral and Social Science Studies)

The rights below are the rights of every person who is asked to be in a research study. As a research subject, you have the following rights:

(1) To be told what area, subject, or issue is being studied.
(2) To be told what will happen to you and what the procedures are.
(3) To be told about the potential risks or discomforts, if any, of the research.
(4) To be told if you can expect any benefit from participating and, if so, what the benefit might be.
(5) To be allowed to ask any questions concerning the study, both before agreeing to be involved and during the course of the study.
(6) To be told what medical treatment is available if any complications or injuries arise as a result of the research study.
(7) To refuse to participate in the study or to stop participating after the study starts.
(8) To receive your signed and dated copy of this Bill of Rights and the consent form.
(9) To be free of pressure when considering whether you wish to be in the study.

If you have other questions, please ask the researcher or research assistant. In addition, you may contact the Office of Human Research Protection (OHRP), which is concerned with protecting volunteers in research projects. You may reach OHRP by calling (xxx) xxx-xxxx, from 8:00 a.m. to 5:00 p.m., Monday through Friday, or by writing to the Office of Human Research Protection, Ambulatory Care Center - Ellison Building, UCDMC, xx ___ Street, Suite xxxx, Sacramento, California 95817.

Signature
of
Participant_____**Date**_____

Appendix 2. Consent to Participate in a Research Study, University of California, Davis

Title of Study: Cherokee Fishing: The Ethnoecology of Aquatic Resource Use Among the Eastern Band of Cherokee Indians.

Investigators' Name, Department, Telephone Number: Heidi Altman; Departments of Anthropology and Native American Studies; (xxx) xxx-xxxx; Martha Macri, Ph.D., Departments of Anthropology and Native American Studies; (xxx) xxx-xxxx.

PURPOSE

You are being asked to participate in a research study. We hope to learn as much as possible about how Cherokee people have used fishing as means for living historically and and how they continue to do so today. This study includes gathering the names of different fishes and aquatic life in Cherokee, understanding fishing techniques and practices, and investigating traditional methods of preserving fish.

PROCEDURES

If you decide to volunteer, you will be interviewed and asked to answer questions about your knowledge of fish, fishing, fish preservation and other things related to fishing. You may also be asked to identify fish and other aquatic animals or fishing practices with Cherokee words if possible.

RISKS

There are no risks to you for your participation in this study.

BENEFITS

It is possible that you will not benefit directly by participating in this study.

CONFIDENTIALITY

Materials that identify your responses as yours will be accesible only to the researchers. The information that you provide will be incorporated anonymously into the final report. Copies of your responses will be made available to you at your request. No one else will be able to access your responses without your written permission. However, absolute confidentiality cannot be guaranteed, since research documents are not protected from subpoena.

COSTS/COMPENSATION

There is no cost to you beyond the time and effort required to complete the procedure described above, nor will there be any compensation.

RIGHT TO REFUSE OR WITHDRAW

You may refuse to participate in this study. If you decide to participate, you may change your mind about being in the study and quit after the study has started.

QUESTIONS

If you have any questions, please ask us. If you have any additional questions later, Heidi Altman will answer them at xx ___ Road, Asheville, NC 28804, (xxx) xxx-xxxx.

CONSENT

YOUR SIGNATURE, BELOW, WILL INDICATE THAT YOU HAVE DECIDED TO VOLUNTEER AS A RESEARCH SUBJECT AND THAT YOU HAVE READ AND UNDERSTAND THE INFORMATION PROVIDED ABOVE.

Signature of participant or legal representative_____

Date_____

Signature of Investigator_____

Date_____

You will be given a signed and dated copy of this form to keep. You will also be given a copy of the Experimental Subject's Bill of Rights.

Appendix 3. Comparison of Cherokee names for fishes and other aquatic life, bait, practices, etc.

Common name	Cherokee (Jerry Wolfe)	Cherokee (Charles Taylor)	Cherokee (M. Bradley)	Cherokee Mooney (1900a)	Cherokee King (1975)
Fish					
fish	ajat	a-tsa-di		aja'di	atsat'i
minnow		a-tsa-di u-ni-tsa-di-ya			
catfish	junich tanal	u-ha-nu-lv-sv a-tsa-di		julisdanali	tsulistanali
sculpin	junigajana vnvtsts	u-na-nv-tsa-dv tsu-ni-lo-di		jisgwalvna adaja	tsiskwalvna umhnvtsathi
little brook trout		a-tsa-di tsu-ni-lo-di	tsulokt		tsunilolhti
rainbow trout	junilashga umahnvjvti	wo-ti-ge-i			
brown trout	vnoliga	o-li-ga	o:li:kh	oliga	olika
redhorse (black) (sicklefin)	junadihlgi				
warpaint shiner	umihtaluga	u-ni-ta-lu-gi a-tsa-di			
central stoneroller	junigachayisht		tv(n)-ka-lvn-atsati:ya	tsvnigitsiyvnsti ajadiya (salmon)	tsunikitsiyvnsti atsvntiya (minnow)
river chub	ajadiyv	u-s-di-tsa-di-ya			
rosyside dace	gigage				

tennessee shiner	junsti ajati				taloke
hogsucker	daloge	da-lo-ge-i		daloge	uhnohka
largemouth bass	utan uhnak	u-no-tse	taloki	unoga	
smallmouth bass	aniyaloge	uninak		unoga	
sunfish	vniagal	ni-go-lv	ukol	agola, anigola	ukolv
mtn brook lamprey	janush			thvdegwa	thlvtekwa
Bait					
helgramite	vnigvnauch	sga-lna a-ni-da			tska'yi
yellowjacket larvae	shku	gan-s-di a-di-g-ti			
stick bait		ts-go-v			
night crawler		to-hla-li-d-s-gi			
grasshopper	talichk^w	ta-la-du-hi			
hornet grubs	shawo^n deh				
crickets					
bread	gadu				
corn	selu				
Reptiles, amphibians, shellfish, and others					
bullfrog	kanunu		ka:nu:nu		
frog	wvlosi				wvlosi
tadpole		ti-li-gi-da		tikitsi	
turkey frog	gwauk				gwvlga

Continued on the next page

Appendix 3. *Continued*

Common name	Cherokee (Jerry Wolfe)	Cherokee (Charles Taylor)	Cherokee (M. Bradley)	Cherokee Mooney (1900a)	Cherokee King (1975)
tree frog	*te^{n}k^{h}*				*tehga*
knee deeps	*dukstu^{n}*			*tustu*	*dusdu*
turtles					
box turtle	*dakshi*			*takshi*	
mud turtle	*shvligug*	*sa-li-gu-ga*	*seli:kuk*		*saligugi*
salamanders					
spring lizard	*dowekh*	*da-we-ga*	*tawekh*	*tuwekha*	*duweka*
water dog		*a-tsu-wa*		*tsuwa*	*thsuwa*
crawfish					
green	*jistvn*	*tsi-s-dv-i*	*tsi:stvn*		*jisdvna*
red	*jishgawgilh*		*tsistakuvalv*		*jisgagili*
leech	*tsanusi*	*tsa-nu-si*			*tsanusi*
water beetle					*tsanusi*
water spider		*u-ni-si-yi ka-na-ni-i-s-gi*			*toyunisi*
Types of water					
swift	*gaulichtayv*	*u-so-nv a-ma-ye-li*		*kolistayvi*	
rough	*dugajinvkshv*	*u-s-ga-no-lv a-ma-ye-li*			
still					

deep	akstigv	u-ta-nv ha-wi-ni a-m-a-ye-li
shallow		u-sa-ge-i a-ma-ye-li
sandy		no-la-hi-yu
muddy		su-wo-da-ha a-ma-ye-li

Phrases related to fishing

fisherman		a-tsa-di a-su-hv-s-di-s-gi
have gutted the fish	dujulvgishv	
have scaled the fish	duhnugaushv	
fish soup	ajat ugum	
to fry fish	digvnvlht ajat	
I am going fishing	dv ga tsu ane'si	ahtshuhv (to fish)

Items of material culture

fish basket	agvhlo	ta-lu-tsa ga-ni-ya a-tsa-di
rivercane	ihiya	ihyv

Continued on the next page

Appendix 3. *Continued*

Common name	Cherokee (Jerry Wolfe)	Cherokee (Charles Taylor)	Cherokee (M. Bradley)	Cherokee Mooney (1900a)	Cherokee King (1975)
pole	*gvdv*				*katvti*
___ fish	*unastagvhit*				
	ajat				
fish hook		*a-su-di*			*atsu'ii*
sinker		*da-no-yv-sv*			
blow guns					*thu'kwehsti*

Appendix 4. Fish known to be on the Qualla Boundary

Common name	Scientific name

Lampreys
mountain brook lamprey · *Ichthyomyzon greeleyi*

Herrings
gizzard shad · *Dorosoma cepedianum*
threadfin shad · *Dorosoma petenense*

Carps and minnows
central stoneroller · *Campostoma anomalum*
rosyside dace · *Clinostomus funduloides*
whitetail shiner · *Cyprinella galactura*
spotfin chub · *C. monacha*
warpaint shiner · *Luxilus coccogenis*
river chub · *Nocomis micropogon*
golden shiner · *Notemigonus crysoleucas*
tennessee shiner · *Notropis leuciodus*
silver shiner · *N. photogenis*
rosyface shiner · *N. rubellus*
mirror shiner · *N. spectrunculus*
telescope shiner · *N. telescopus*
mimic shiner · *N. volucellus*
fatlips minnow · *Phenacobius crassilabrum*
blacknose dace · *Rhinichthys atratulus*
longnose dace · *R. cataractae*
creek chub · *Semotilus atromaculatus*

Suckers
white sucker · *Catostomus commersoni*
northern hog sucker · *Hypentelium nigricans*
silver redhorse · *Moxostoma anisurum*
river redhorse · *M. carinatum*
sicklefin redhorse · *M. sp. (undescribed)*
black redhorse · *M. duquesnei*
golden redhorse · *M. erythrurum*
shorthead redhorse · *M. macrolepidotum*

Continued on the next page

Appendix 4. *Continued*

Common name	Scientific name
Bullhead cats	
channel catfish	*Ictalurus punctatus*
flathead catfish	*Pylodictus olivaris*
Pikes	
northern pike	*Esox lucius*
Trouts	
rainbow trout	*Oncorhynchus mykiss*
brown trout	*Salmo trutta*
brook trout	*Salvelinus fontinalis*
Sculpins	
mottled sculpin	*Cottus bairdi*
Sunfishes	
rock bass	*Ambloplites rupestris*
redbreast sunfish	*Lepomis auritus*
bluegill	*L. macrochirus*
smallmouth bass	*Micropterus dolomieu*
largemouth bass	*M. salmoides*
spotted bass	*M. punctulatus*
Perches	
greenside darter	*Etheostoma blennoides*
greenfin darter	*E. chlorobranchium*
wounded darter	*E. vulneratum*
banded darter	*E. zonale*
tangerine darter	*Percina aurantiaca*
gilt darter	*P. evides*
olive darter	*P. squamata*

Adapted from Rohde et al. (1994), and narrowed to Swain County with information from Mehinnick (1991).

Appendix 5. Fishing practices, items of material culture, and their associations with particular fish

Fishing method	Associated Cherokee words	Associated material culture	Fish caught with this method	Sources
Blowgun	Blowgun *tukwehsti*	Rivercane blowgun and projectiles	Large fish (e.g., trout, redhorse, hogsuckers)	Adair
Bow and arrow		Bow and arrow	Large fish (e.g., trout, redhorse, hogsuckers)	Adair, Speck
Dragging		Vine nets or drags, modified trees or bushes	Various (including large and small fish)	Speck
Fish poisoning	"They (the fish) are in a state of dizziness" *uniyashtigishti* Fish basket (large type) *agvhlo* Fish basket *ta-lu-tsa ga-ni-ya a-tsa-di* Dip basket *akugist taluja* Walnut *shed*	Processed vegetal poisons, fish baskets, sifter baskets, temporary dams or weirs	Various (including large and small fish)	Adair, Speck, interviews
Harpoons and gigs	Spear or gig *gatsiohdstvdodi* Canoe *tsi-yu*	Green cane or wood harpoons, dugout canoes	Large fish (e.g., trout, redhorse, hogsuckers; Adair mentions sturgeon specifically)	Adair

Continued on the next page

Appendix 5. *Continued*

Fishing method	Associated Cherokee words	Associated material culture	Fish caught with this method	Sources
Hook and line	Rivercane *ihiya* Pole *gvdv* Hook *a-su-di* Line *ah-s-di a-tsa-di* Sinker *da-no-yv-sv* Leader *wadun*	Traditionally bone hooks, Contact period horsehair line, bent pin hooks, Contemporary commercially available rods, reels, lures and hooks	Trout, bass, sunfish	Adair, Speck, Mooney, interviews
Seining		Nets made from tow sacks joined together and attached to a wooden frame	Various (including large and small fish)	Interviews
Snaring	"I was snaring them" *Gujeya ishdishkla*	Commercially available treble hooks and line	Stoneroller, Redhorse, Hogsucker	Interviews
Trapping	Basket trap *agayvtv* "They have a trap set" *Uniagayvtv*	Woven basket traps, bushes and trees modified into traps	Various (including large and small fish)	
Trotline		Commerically available line and hooks	Redhorse	Speck, interviews
Weirs		Stone obstructions constructed across rivers	Various (including large and small fish)	Timberlake

The Cherokee words were provided by Jerry Wolfe and Charles Taylor in interviews.

Appendix 6. Glosses of names of species of fish identified by Cherokee speakers today

Common name	Cherokee name	Gloss	Local English vernacular
fish	atsat'i	n/a	n/a
minnow	amakta	n/a	n/a
river chub, minnow	atsatiya	'principal fish'	knotty head, redbelly
hogsucker	taloke	n/a	n/a
redhorse (golden)	olika	n/a	n/a
(sicklefin)	junadihlgi	'it wears a feather'	n/a
brook trout	unhnvtsathi	'speckled'	Speckled trout, brookie
rainbow trout	tsunilolhti	n/a	n/a
brown trout	wotikei unahnvjvti	'brown' 'speckled fish'	Speckled trout
central stoneroller	tsunikitsiyvnsti	'it is pushing it around'	flutterfish (spawning), mumblehead
largemouth bass	uhnohka	'big bass'	bass
smallmouth bass	aniyaloge uninak	'small bass'	bass
sunfish	ukolv	n/a	n/a
rosyside dace	gigage	'red'	n/a
tennessee shiner	junsti ajati	'little fish'	silversides
warpaint shiner	unihtaluga	'it looks like metal'	silversides
sculpin	tsiskwalvna	'it has been hit in the head'	mallet head
channel catfish	tsulistanali	'(whiskers) blow-ing in the breeze'	blue catfish
mtn brook lamprey	thlvtekwa	n/a	eel

Notes

Chapter 2

1. Changing subsistence practices are discussed in detail in Chapter 3.

2. The traditional belief system is reflective of the core of these values. Chapter 4 features a discussion of traditional Cherokee beliefs and values generally and as they specifically pertain to fishing.

3. Thornton provides an extensive discussion of population estimates and arrives at a figure for population loss through disease of nearly 47 percent from precontact times to 1800. Subsequent population gains were made in the Southeast among the Cherokee and other groups through out-marriage and other means of survival. See Thornton 1990 and Paredes and Plante (1982) for more complete discussions of the ebb and flow of the Cherokee demographic during the postcontact period.

4. Although this change has moved individual interests away from the day-to-day management of farms, hunting, fishing, and gathering for subsistence, it has allowed for the development of leisure fishing, which reflects a reevaluation of the role of fishing in Cherokee ethnic identity. In Chapter 5, I examine the role of the environment in fishing as a tourist enterprise and the ways in which Cherokee identity is constructed relative to fishing practices, tribal waters, and the development of fishing-related tourism.

5. Aboriginal population estimates vary widely depending on a number of factors, most important the method used to reach the estimate. See Thornton (1990) for a thorough discussion of Cherokee aboriginal population estimates.

6. The deerskin trade and dependency theory in the Southeast (particularly among the Choctaw) are discussed in White (1983).

7. Chapter 4 contains a more detailed discussion of "going to water" and its relationship to beliefs about water.

8. Timberlake's description of fishing practices is presented in Chapter 3.

9. Certainly Cherokee women of Timberlake's time would have been amused at his comment that the land is "so remarkably fertile, that the women alone do all

the laborious tasks of agriculture, the soil requiring only a little stirring with a hoe to produce whatever is required of it" (Williams 1927:68).

10. The notion of traditional knowledge of the environment, its persistence, and its adaptability is a central part of the discussion in Chapter 4.

11. For a fascinating discussion of class and racial dynamics among the Cherokee of this period, see Miles (2005).

12. Appendix 4 lists the common name and the scientific name of the fish that have been documented in the Swain County area. The county is bordered by the Fontana Lake reservoir on its western edge, so some species shown as present in the county are not necessarily known to speakers who fish predominantly on the Qualla Boundary.

13. Tourism and its relationship to fishing are explored in Chapter 5.

14. The Hunter and the Dagwa is a clear example of the diffusion of tales from the Bible (Jonah and the whale) or classical antiquity (Hercules). Knowledge of or belief in sea monsters in the interior Southeast seems unlikely. However, Cherokee folklore does make mention of other kinds of malevolent creatures in the water. See, for example, the discussion of leeches in Chapter 4.

Chapter 3

1. Appendix 5 lists the methods of fishing documented by this research, along with the material culture associated with each method, the types of fish caught with each method, and the sources where the method was mentioned.

2. For further information on the archaeology of the Overhill Cherokee and the cultures that preceded the Cherokee in east Tennessee, see the series of volumes titled *University of Tennessee Department of Anthropology Report of Investigations,* produced in conjunction with the Tennessee Valley Authority.

3. For a discussion of fishing formulae, see Chapter 4.

4. For example, while voicing is not commonly a distinctive feature within any of the dialects of Cherokee—e.g., [g] and [k] are allophones—it is an aspect of dialectal variation among Eastern, Snowbird, and Western dialects. Similarly, voiced and voiceless alternants [t] and [d] and [ts] and [j] also mark dialectal rather than phonemic boundaries. Mooney uses only the voiced consonants, which are reflected most often in transcriptions of the syllabary, whereas King uses only the unvoiced consonants, which could possibly reflect transcriptions of oral data from speakers of the Kituwah dialect.

Chapter 4

1. Mooney's work stands as the most complete examination of Cherokee history, customs, and belief. His *Myths and Sacred Formulas of the Cherokee* (1900a) reports on an extended period of fieldwork in North Carolina in the 1890s, a time that was one generation after the Removal when the culture was adapting to its aftereffects. After Mooney's death, Franz Olbrechts completed the interpretation and

analysis of *The Swimmer Manuscript: Cherokee Sacred Formulas and Medicinal Prescriptions* (1932), which Mooney had begun. *The Swimmer Manuscript* includes a critical analysis of what is purported to be the notebook of one medicine man, Ayunini or Swimmer, obtained by Mooney during his fieldwork in the Eastern Cherokee community.

2. The color and cardinal direction symbolism are characteristic of traditional Cherokee medicine. According to Mooney and Olbrechts (1932:43–44), there are seven sacred colors mentioned in the formulae (black, white, brown, blue, purple, red, and yellow); the four cardinal directions plus "on high," "in the center," and "above" are noted as the locations of spirits; and 4, 7, and 12 (or possibly 24) are sacred numbers that govern the administration of the formulae and other aspects of traditional medicine.

3. These include formulae to "outdo a rival fisherman," to "inspirit a fish-hook," to "catch all kinds of fish," to "catch a large fish," and several to "inspirit a fish trap." There is a table of contents in Mooney's own hand that states that 9 of the original 22 formulae were for use in fishing. Unfortunately, none of them include the translations, glossaries, botanical information, or annotations promised in the table of contents. There are also apparently unrelated materials in the manuscript, including translations of letters and other notes (Mooney n.d.).

Chapter 6

1. Robert Jenkins, Ph.D., Roanoke College, the leading researcher on sucker fishes in this area, has recently produced some of the first scientific descriptions of this particular species of redhorse.

Bibliography

The Springplace Diaries, 1814, 1825, 1827. Springplace Mission, Georgia. Located in the Moravian Archives. Winston-Salem, North Carolina.

Adair, James
1775   The history of the American Indians, particularly those nations adjoining to the Missisippi, East and West Florida, Georgia, South and North Carolina, and Virginia: containing an account of their origin, language, manners, religious and civil customs, laws, form of government, punishments, conduct in war and domestic life, their habits, diet, agriculture, manufactures, diseases and method of cure . . . with observations on former historians, the conduct of our colony governors, superintendents, missionaries, &c. Also an appendix, containing a description of the Floridas, and the Missisippi lands, with their productions—The benefits of colonizing Georgiana, and civilizing the Indians—And the way to make all the colonies more valuable to the Mother Country. London: E. and C. Dilly.

Altman, Heidi
1997   Caught Me a Big 'Un: Fish Tales and Southern Male Discourse. Symposium about Language and Society Austin V (SALSA V), Austin, Texas, March 12, 1997.

Barton, Benjamin Smith
1797   New Views of the Origin of the Tribes and Nations of America. Philadelphia: John Bioren. Facsimile reprint, Millwood, N.Y.: Kraus, 1976.

Bartram, William
1793   Travels through North and South Carolina, Georgia, East and West Florida, the Cherokee country, the extensive territories of the Muscogulges, or Creek confederacy, and the country of the Chactaws; containing an account of the soil and natural productions of those regions; together with observations on the manners of the Indians. Dublin: For J. Moore, W. Jones, R. McAllister and J. Rice.

Bashkow, Ira
2004   A Neo-Boasian Conception of Cultural Boundaries. American Anthropologist 106(3):443–458.

Basso, Keith

1984   Stalking with Stories: Names, Places and Moral Narratives among the West-
        ern Apache. *In* Text, Play and Story: The Reconstruction of Self and Society.
        E. Bruner, ed. Washington, D.C.: American Anthropological Association.

Bender, Margaret

1996   Reading Culture: The Cherokee Syllabary and the Eastern Cherokees, 1993–
        1995. Ph.D. dissertation, Department of Anthropology, University of Chi-
        cago.

2002   Signs of Cherokee Culture: Sequoyah's Syllabary in Eastern Cherokee Life.
        Chapel Hill: University of North Carolina Press.

Berkes, Firket

1993   Traditional Ecological Knowledge in Perspective. *In* Traditional Ecological
        Knowledge: Concepts and Cases. J. Inglis, ed. Ottawa, Ont.: International
        Program on Traditional Ecological Knowledge and International Develop-
        ment Centre.

Berlin, Brent

1971   Speculations on the Growth of Ethnobotanical Nomenclature. Berkeley:
        University of California Language-Behavior Research Laboratory.

Berlin, Brent, and Paul Kay

1969   Basic Color Terms: Their Universality and Evolution. Berkeley: University
        of California Press.

Boas, Franz

1966a   Introduction to Handbook of American Indian Languages. Lincoln: Uni-
        versity of Nebraska Press.

1966b   Race, Language and Culture. New York: Free Press.

1966c   The Mind of Primitive Man. New York: Free Press.

Braund, Kathryn E. Holland

1993   Deerskins and Duffels: The Creek Indian Trade with Anglo-America, 1685–
        1815. Lincoln: University of Nebraska Press.

Bruner, E., ed.

1984   Text, Play and Story: The Reconstruction of Self and Society. Washing-
        ton, D.C.: American Anthropological Association.

Bunzl, Matti

2004   Boas, Foucault and the "Native Anthropologist": Notes toward a Neo-
        Boasian Anthropology. American Anthropologist 106(3):435–442.

Campbell, Lyle, and Marianne Mithun

1979   The Languages of Native America: Historical and Comparative Assessment.
        Austin: University of Texas Press.

Carroll, John B., ed.

1956   Language, Thought and Reality: Selected Writings of Benjamin Lee Whorf.
        Cambridge: Massachusetts Institute of Technology.

Castiglioni, Luigi, et al.

1983   Luigi Castiglioni's Viaggio: Travels in the United States of North America,
        1785–87. Syracuse, N.Y.: Syracuse University Press.

Chafe, Wallace L.

1976   The Caddoan, Iroquoian and Siouan Languages. The Hague: Mouton.

Chapman, Charlotte Gower

1927   The Northern and Southern Affiliations of Antillean Culture. Menasha, Wis.: Pub. for the American Anthropological Association.

Conklin, Harold C.

1955   Hanuoo Color Categories. Southwestern Journal of Anthropology 11:339–344.

1962   Lexicographical Treatment of Folk Taxonomies. International Journal of American Linguistics 28(2):119–141.

Cook, William Hinton

1979   A Grammar of North Carolina Cherokee. Ph.D. dissertation, Department of Linguistics, Yale University.

Dickens, Roy S., Jr.

1976   Cherokee Prehistory: The Pisgah Phase in the Appalachian Summit Region. Knoxville: University of Tennessee Press.

Douglas, Mary

1966   Purity and Danger: An Analysis of Concept of Pollution and Taboo. London: Routledge and Kegan Paul.

Duggan, Betty J., and Brett H. Riggs

1991   Studies in Cherokee Basketry. Occasional paper of the Frank H. McClung Museum, University of Tennessee. With reprint of Decorative Art and Basketry of the Cherokee by Frank Gouldsmith Speck, 1920.

Duncan, Barbara, and Brett Riggs

2003   Cherokee Heritage Trails. Chapel Hill: University of North Carolina Press.

Eastern Band of Cherokee Indians (EBCI), Department of Game and Fish

n.d.   Fishing Regulations. Pamphlet.

1972   Cherokee Progress and Challenge. Cherokee, N.C.: EBCI.

1976   Overall Economic Development Plan. Cherokee, N.C.: EBCI.

Feeling, Durbin, and William Pulte

1975   Cherokee-English Dictionary. [Tahlequah]: Cherokee Nation of Oklahoma.

Fenton, William Nelson, and John Gulick

1961   Symposium on Cherokee and Iroquois Culture. Paper presented at the 58th AAA meetings, Mexico City, 1959. Bureau of American Ethnology Bulletin. Washington, D.C.: Smithsonian Institution.

Finger, John R.

1984   The Eastern Band of Cherokees, 1819–1900. Knoxville: University of Tennessee Press.

1991   Cherokee Americans: The Eastern Band of Cherokees in the Twentieth Century. Lincoln: University of Nebraska Press.

Fogelson, Raymond

1961   Change, Persistence, and Accommodation in Cherokee Medico-Magical Beliefs. In Symposium on Cherokee and Iroquois Culture. W. N. Fenton and J. Gulick, eds. Pp. 215–225. Bureau of American Ethnology Bulletin 180. Washington, D.C.: Smithsonian Institution.

1990   On the "Petticoat Government" of the Eighteenth Century Cherokees. *In* Personality in the Cultural Construction of Society: Papers in Honor of Melford E. Spiro. D. K. Jordan, ed. Tuscaloosa: University of Alabama Press.

Fogelson, Raymond, and Paul Kutsche

1961   Cherokee Economic Cooperatives: The Gadugi. *In* Symposium on Cherokee and Iroquois Culture. W. N. Fenton and J. Gulick, eds. Pp. 87–121. Bulletin 180. Washington, D.C.: Smithsonian Institution, Bureau of American Ethnology.

Fradkin, Arlene

1990   Cherokee Folk Zoology: The Animal World of a Native American People, 1700–1838. New York: Garland.

Frake, Charles

1961   The Diagnosis of Disease among the Subanun of Mindanao. American Anthropologist 63:113–132.

1964   Notes on Queries in Ethnography. American Anthropologist 66(3):132–145.

1969   The Ethnographic Study of Cognitive Systems. *In* Cognitive Anthropology. S. A. Tyler, ed. Pp. 28–41. New York: Holt, Rinehart and Winston.

French, Laurence

1998   The Qualla Cherokee Surviving in Two Worlds. Lewiston, N.Y.: E. Mellen Press.

Gallatin, Albert

1836   A Synopsis of the Indian tribes within the United States East of the Rocky Mountains, and in the British and Russian Possessions in North America. Transactions and Collections of the American Antiquarian Society, Cambridge, Mass.

Gilbert, William Harlen

1934   Eastern Cherokee Social Organization. Ph.D. dissertation, Department of Anthropology, University of Chicago.

Gleeson, Paul F., and Tennessee Valley Authority

1970   Archaeological Investigations in the Tellico Reservoir: Interim Report, 1969. Knoxville: Department of Anthropology, University of Tennessee.

Goodwin, Gary C.

1977   Cherokees in Transition: A Study of Changing Culture and Environment Prior to 1775. Chicago: Department of Geography, University of Chicago.

Gulick, John

1960   Cherokees at the Crossroads. Chapel Hill: Institute for Research in Social Science, University of North Carolina.

1973   Cherokees at the Crossroads. Expanded ed. Chapel Hill: Institute for Research in Social Science, University of North Carolina.

Gumperz, John Joseph, and Stephen C. Levinson

1996   Rethinking Linguistic Relativity. Cambridge and New York: Cambridge University Press.

Handler, Richard

2004   Afterword: Mysteries of Culture. American Anthropologist 106(3):488–494.

Hardesty, Donald L.

1977   Ecological Anthropology. New York: Wiley.

Harrington, M. R.

1922   Cherokee and Earlier Remains on the Upper Tennessee River. New York: Museum of the American Indian, Heye Foundation.

Hatley, M. Thomas

1995   The Dividing Paths: Cherokees and South Carolinians Through the Era of Revolution. New York: Oxford University Press.

Hill, Sarah H.

1997   Weaving New Worlds: Southeastern Cherokee Women and Their Basketry. Chapel Hill: University of North Carolina Press.

Hockett, Charles

1977   The View from Language: Selected Essays, 1948–1974. Athens: University of Georgia Press.

Hudson, Charles M.

1982   The Southeastern Indians. Knoxville: University of Tennessee Press.

Inglis, Julian, ed.

1993   Traditional Ecological Knowledge: Concepts and Cases. Ottawa, Ont.: International Program on Traditional Ecological Knowledge and International Development Research Centre.

Jafari, Jafar

2001   The Scientification of Tourism. In Hosts and Guests Revisited. V. Smith and M. Brent, eds. Pp. 28–41. New York: Cognizant Communication Corporation.

Kay, Paul, and C. K. McDaniel

1978   The Linguistic Significance of the Meanings of Basic Color Terms. Language 54:610–646.

King, Duane H.

1975   A Grammar and Dictionary of the Cherokee Language. Ph.D. dissertation, Department of Anthropology, University of Georgia.

1977   Lessons in Cherokee Ethnology from the Captivity of Joseph Brown, 1788–1789. Journal of Cherokee Studies 2(2):219–229.

1979   The Cherokee Indian Nation: A Troubled History. Knoxville: University of Tennessee Press.

King, Laura Hill

1977   The Cherokee Storyteller: The Red and Green Crayfish. Journal of Cherokee Studies 2(2):246–249.

Krech, Shepard

1999   The Ecological Indian: Myth and History. New York: W. W. Norton.

Kupferer, Harriet J.

1966   The "Principal People," 1960: A Study of Cultural and Social Groups of the Eastern Cherokee. Washington, D.C.: USGPO.

Littlejohn, Margaret

1997   Great Smoky Mountains National Park Visitor Studies, Summer and Fall 1996. Visitor Services Project Report 92, Cooperative Park Studies Unit.

Lounsbury, Floyd

1961   Iroquois-Cherokee Relations. *In* Symposium on Cherokee and Iroquois Culture. W. N. Fenton, and J. Gulick, eds. Bulletin 180. Washington, D.C.: Smithsonian Institution, Bureau of American Ethnology.

Lucy, John Arthur

1992a   Grammatical Categories and Cognition: A Case Study of the Linguistic Relativity Hypothesis. Cambridge and New York: Cambridge University Press.

1992b   Language Diversity and Thought: A Reformulation of the Linguistic Relativity Hypothesis. Cambridge and New York: Cambridge University Press.

1996   The Scope of Linguistic Relativity. *In* Rethinking Linguistic Relativity. J. J. Gumperz and S. Levinson, eds. Studies in the Social and Cultural Foundations of Language, 17:37–69. Cambridge, Eng.: Cambridge University Press.

Maffi, Luisa

2001   On Biocultural Diversity: Linking Language, Knowledge, and the Environment. Washington, D.C.: Smithsonian Institution Press.

Malainey, M. E., with R. Przybylski and B. L. Sherriff

2001   One Person's Food: How and Why Fish Avoidance May Affect the Settlement Patterns of Hunter-Gatherers. American Antiquity 66(1):141–161.

Maney, Kenneth

2002   Interview and Tour of Cherokee Fish Hatchery. Cherokee, N.C.

Martin, Calvin

1978   Keepers of the Game: Indian-Animal Relationships and the Fur Trade. Berkeley: University of California Press.

McLoughlin, William Gerald

1984   Cherokees and Missionaries, 1789–1839. New Haven: Yale University Press.

Mehinnick, Edward F.

1991   Freshwater Fishes of North Carolina. Charlotte: North Carolina Wildlife Resources Commission.

Metzger, Duane G., and Gerald E. Williams

1966   Some Procedures and Results in the Study of Native Categories: Tzeltal "Firewood." American Anthropologist 63:113–132.

Miles, Tiya

2005   Ties that Bind: The Story of an Afro-Cherokee Family in Slavery and Freedom. American Crossroads Series 14. Berkeley: University of California Press.

Mithun, Marianne

1999   The Languages of Native North America. Cambridge and New York: Cambridge University Press.

Mooney, James

1891   The Sacred Formulas of the Cherokees. Bulletin 17. Washington, D.C.: Smithsonian Institution, Bureau of American Ethnology.

1900a   Myths of the Cherokee. Bulletin 19. Washington: Smithsonian Institution, Bureau of American Ethnology.

1900b   The Cherokee River Cult. Journal of American Folklore 13(48):1–10.
n.d.   Manuscript 2278, p. 26, Smithsonian Institution National Anthropological Archives: Cherokee Sacred Formulae for Hunting and Fishing. In Numbered manuscripts, 1850s–1890s (some earlier). Washington, D.C.
Mooney, James, and Frans M. Olbrechts
1932   The Swimmer Manuscript: Cherokee Sacred Formulas and Medicinal Prescriptions. Washington, D.C.: USGPO.
Nabhan, Gary
2001   Cultural Perceptions of Ecological Interactions. In On Biocultural Diversity. L. Maffi, ed. Pp. 145–156. Washington, D.C.: Smithsonian Institution Press.
Neely, Sharlotte
1991   Snowbird Cherokees: People of Persistence. Athens: University of Georgia Press.
Niering, William A., and Nancy C. Olmstead
1979   The Audubon Society Field Guide to North American Wildflowers, Eastern Region. Visual key by Susan Rayfield and Carol Nehring. New York: Knopf; distributed by Random House.
North Carolina Wildlife Resources Commission
n.d.   Brook Trout. North Carolina Wild: Wildlife Profiles.
Orta, Andrew
2004   The Promise of Particularism and the Theology of Culture: Limits and Lessons of "Neo-Boasianism." American Anthropologist 106(3):473–487.
Paredes, James Anthony
1995   Paradoxes of Modernism and Indianness in the Southeast. American Indian Quarterly 19(3):341–360.
Paredes, J. Anthony, and Kenneth J. Plante.
1982   A Reexamination of Creek Indian Population Trends, 1738–1832. American Indian Culture and Research Journal 6(4):3–28.
Perdue, Theda
1998   Cherokee Women: Gender and Culture Change, 1700–1835. Lincoln: University of Nebraska Press.
Pilling, James Constantine
1888   Bibliography of the Iroquoian Languages. Bureau of American Ethnology Bulletin 6. Washington, D.C.: Smithsonian Institution.
Posey, Darrell Addison
2001   Biological and Cultural Diverstiy: The Inextricable, Linked by Language and Politics. In On Biocultural Diversity. L. Maffi, ed. Pp. 379–396. Washington, D.C.: Smithsonian Institution Press.
Posey, Darrell Addison, and J. Slikerveer
1999   Cultural and Spiritual Values of Biodiversity. United Nations Environment Programme. London: Intermediate Technology.
Ranjel, Rodrigo
1993   Account of the Northern Conquest and Discovery of Hernando DeSoto. In The DeSoto Chronicles. Lawrence A. Clayton, Vernon J. Knight, and

Edward C. Moore, eds. Pp. 247–306. Tuscaloosa: University of Alabama Press. (First published in Spanish, 1851; first published in English, 1904.)

Riggs, Brett H.

1999   Removal Period Cherokee Households in Southwestern North Carolina: Material Perspectives on Ethnicity and Cultural Differentiation. Ph.D. dissertaion, Department of Anthropology, University of Tennessee.

Rogers, Anne

1993   Fish Weirs as Part of the Cultural Landscape. Appalachian Cultural Resources Workshop, 1993. National Park Service, Southeast Regional Office, Cultural Resources Planning Division.

Rohde, Fred C., et al.

1996   Freshwater Fishes of the Carolinas, Virginia, Maryland, and Delaware. Chapel Hill: University of North Carolina Press.

Rohde, Fred C., et al.

1994   Freshwater Fishes of the Carolinas, Virginia, Maryland, and Delaware. Chapel Hill: University of North Carolina Press.

Rosenblatt, Daniel

2004   An Anthropology Made Safe for Culture: Patterns of Practice and the Politics of Difference in Ruth Benedict. American Antrhopologist 106(3): 459–472.

Sabella, James C.

1980   José Olaya: Analysis of a Peruvian Fishing Cooperative that Failed. Anthropological Quarterly 53:56–63.

Sapir, Edward

1964   Culture, Language and Personality: Selected Essays. Berkeley: University of California Press.

Saussure, Ferdinand de

1983   Course in General Linguistics. Charles Bally and Albert Sechehaye, eds., in
[1916] collaboration with Albert Reidlinger. Translated from the French by Wade Baskin. New York: McGraw-Hill.

Scancarelli, Janine

1987   Grammatical Relations and Verb Agreement in Cherokee. Ph.D. dissertation, Department of Linguistics, UCLA.

Schroedl, Gerald F., with James F. Bates and the Tennessee Valley Authority

1986   Overhill Cherokee Archaeology at Chota-Tanasee. Chattanooga: Tennessee Valley Authority.

Silverstein, Michael

1976   Shifters, Linguistic Categories and Cultural Description. *In* Meaning in Anthropology. K. Basso, ed. Pp. 11–55. Albuquerque: University of New Mexico Press.

Silverstein, Michael, and Greg Urban

1996   Natural Histories of Discourse. Chicago: University of Chicago Press.

Smith, Valene

2001   Tourism Change and Impacts. *In* Hosts and Guests Revisited: Tourism Issues of the 21st Century. V. Smith and M. Brent, eds. Pp. 107–121. New York: Cognizant Communication Corporation.

Smith, Valene L., and Maryann Brent

2001 Hosts and Guests Revisited: Tourism Issues of the 21st Century. New York: Cognizant Communication Corporation.

Speck, Frank Gouldsmith

1946 Catawba Hunting, Trapping and Fishing. Philadelphia: University Museum.

Stocking, George W., Jr., ed.

1974 The Shaping of American Anthropology, 1883–1911, a Franz Boas Reader. New York: Basic Books.

Swanton, John Reed

1979 The Indians of the Southeastern United States. Bureau of American Ethnology 137. Classics in Smithsonian Anthropology 2. Washington: Smithsonian Institution Press.

Tennessee Valley Authority

2002 Tennessee Valley Authority homepage, www.tva.com.

Thompson, Angie

2002 Talking Trees Children's Fishing Derby. In Cumberland Stories. Cherokee, N.C.: ESPN2.

Thornton, Russell

1990 The Cherokees: A Population History. Lincoln: University of Nebraska Press.

U.S. Environmental Protection Agency

2002 Enviromapper http://map2.epa.gov/enviromapper.

U.S. Geological Survey

2002 Water Resources of Tennessee, http://www.tn.water.usgs.gov.

U.S. National Park Service

1981 Great Smoky Mountains National Park Guidebook. Vol. 112. Washington, D.C.: U.S. Department of the Interior.

2002 Great Smoky Mountains National Park: Park Facts, http://www.nps.gov/grsm.

Wallace, Anthony C. F.

1965 The Problem of the Psychological Validity of Componential Analyses. American Anthropologist 67(5):229–248.

White, John K.

1962 On the Revival of Printing in the Cherokee Language. Current Anthropology 3:511–514.

White, Richard

1983 The Roots of Dependency. Lincoln: University of Nebraska Press.

Williams, Michael Ann

1995 Great Smoky Mountains Folklife. Jackson: University Press of Mississippi.

Williams, Samuel Cole

1927 The memoirs of Lieut. Henry Timberlake: (who accompanied the three Cherokee Indians to England in the year 1762); containing whatever he observed remarkable, or worthy of public notice, during his travels to and from that nation; wherein the country, government, genius, and customs of the inhabitants, are authentically described; also the principal occurences during their residence in London; illustrated with an accurate map of their Over-hill settlement, and a curious secret journal, taken by the Indians out of the pocket of a Frenchman they had killed. Johnson City, Tenn.: Watauga Press.

Witthoft, John

n.d.   "A Cherokee Economic Botany from Western North Carolina." In the holdings of the American Philosophical Society (497.3 Am4 No. 4).

Index